ADVENTURE
REVOLUTION

Belinda Kirk is an explorer and the leading campaigner promoting the benefits of adventure on wellbeing. For the past twenty-five years, she has led dozens of international expeditions and remote filming trips. Belinda has walked through Nicaragua, sailed across the Atlantic, searched for camels in China's Desert of Death, discovered ancient rock paintings in Lesotho and gained a Guinness World Record for rowing unsupported around Britain. She has led numerous youth development challenges, pioneered inclusive expeditions for people with disabilities and managed scientific research missions in the Amazon, Sinai and Alaska. In 2009, Belinda established Explorers Connect, a non-profit organisation connecting people to adventure and has encouraged 30,000 ordinary people to engage in outdoor challenges. In 2020 she launched the first conference to explore the Adventure Effect, the positive impact that adventurous activity has on wellbeing.

ADVENTURE REVOLUTION

THE LIFE-CHANGING POWER OF CHOOSING CHALLENGE

BELINDA KIRK

PIATKUS

PIATKUS

First published in Great Britain in 2021 by Piatkus

1 3 5 7 9 10 8 6 4 2

A CIP catalogue record for this book
is available from the British Library.

ISBN: 978-0-349-42823-9

Typeset in Bembo by Hewer Text UK Ltd, Edinburgh
Printed and bound in Great Britain by Clays Ltd, Elcograf S.p.A.

Papers used by Piatkus are from well-managed forests and other responsible sources.

Piatkus
An imprint of
Little, Brown Book Group
Carmelite House
50 Victoria Embankment
London EC4Y 0DZ

An Hachette UK Company
www.hachette.co.uk

www.littlebrown.co.uk

To Jackson

My greatest adventure

Contents

Introduction

Nineteen years ago, everything changed. It was the day I realised that adventure is not a frivolous luxury but a necessity of the human spirit.

I was standing in the rain outside the iconic Royal Geographical Society (RGS) in London. During the previous summer of 2002, I had led a group of young people through the Amazon, and we had reconvened to present our findings. I was just twenty-six years old – the youngest Chief Leader the British Exploring Society (BES) had ever let lead this kind of expedition. I had nearly a decade of experience on my own, but I still had a lot to learn. Although I'd experienced my own personal transformation as a result of adventuring, I had no appreciation of the kind of impact adventurous activity could have on other people. As I waited, a woman approached me.

'What did you do to my daughter?' she asked.

I panicked for a moment, a whole host of scenarios running through my head. There was the girl who'd been bitten by a bat. Could it have been her? Maybe she was part of the team that missed their resupply and had to subsist on nothing but tinned sardines for two days? Or maybe she was one of the unlucky few who experienced the joy of jungle parasites?

Before I could say anything, the woman gave me a giant bear hug, like we were long lost friends. 'I don't recognise her,' she said. 'She's a different girl. She's so much happier. I can't thank you enough.' She told me her daughter was Alice, and then it clicked. Alice had been one of my toughest challenges of the trip. A seventeen-year-old with low self-confidence and a history of self-harm, Alice struggled – mentally, academically and socially. While most of the team formed fast friendships, when we first set out Alice was distant. Friends didn't come easy, it seemed, and she wasn't connecting well with the rest of the group. I tried a few different tactics to bring her into the fold, but nothing seemed to work. So, I gave her a job.

I put Alice in charge of the group kit for her team of twelve. Basically, she was responsible for ensuring the team was equipped with the right gear. It was an important job – and one that would require her to talk to every member of the team. At first, I helped her. I didn't want her to panic or become more fearful. But little by little, Alice owned the role. I could see she was smart and capable – and eventually, so could she.

A few weeks into the expedition, I visited Alice's team. They had been moving around the jungle but had set up camp for a few days to assemble bat netting and carry out biological surveys. When I found them, I was pleased to discover that Alice had volunteered to be the camp manager, running the day-to-day logistics of their basecamp. The timid girl I had met at the airport just a few weeks earlier was now confidently striding about *her* jungle camp, arranging water-purification checks, making cooking schedules and assigning work rotations. I almost didn't recognise her.

From the outside, it was impossible to miss the transformation. The girl who had joined the expedition and the young woman who'd returned to her family in Britain were strikingly different. But I'd never considered how deep a transformation it could prove to be – and how long it might last once she was out of the jungle. And yet, six months later, here was her mother, hugging me in the rain, telling me that Alice now helped out at home, had brought her grades up and, perhaps most importantly, even had a few new friends.

For all my memories of that trip – the boat that sank, the Toyota I rolled on a jungle track, and all the wonderful young people – I'll never forget this one interaction outside the RGS. It seems as clear today as it was the day after it happened. I believe that it's so seared into my memory because it was the moment I came to fully believe in the power of adventure to change people's lives for the better. Before being embraced by Alice's mum, adventure was simply a fix for me – my way of escaping myself and feeling most alive, hooked like an addict, always searching for the next challenge. Yet, since that moment, my focus has shifted from the next expansive jungle, big mountain or open ocean to the many ways that I can make a positive impact on the world, with adventure as the way.

Adventure changed my life. And for the last twenty-six years of taking others on adventurous activities, I have seen it change people of all ages and abilities, and from all walks of life – seen it turn the timid into the confident, the addicted into the recovering and the lost into the intentionally wandering. As a force for change, adventure can be powerful like few others. But the day I met Alice's mum was the day I asked myself the question I can't stop asking: how can we harness the transformational power of adventure, both for ourselves and for others? And this is what *Adventure Revolution* is all about. We'll journey across jungles, up volcanoes and down rivers with people who had a lot to lose but even more to gain from adventure. We'll also camp under the stars close to home and learn to surf or climb for the first time – adventure does not have to be in hostile environments or involve breaking records to count.

We'll meet Amina, a homeless, angry teenager who became an inspiring youth leader. And Freyja, a successful yet unsatis-fied manager who, through climbing, became a proactive, brave woman in charge of her life and career. And Kelvyn, an entrepreneur who was able to use adventure to help him cope with tragic events in his life and now helps others to boost their own wellbeing through adventure. These are normal people, not adrenaline junkies or superhumans.

Since that moment outside the RGS, I've noticed the powerful transformation possible when we answer our inbuilt call to adventure. And I've come to understand the damage caused when we ignore it. We have developed and become boxed in by an always-on synthetic environment that prioritises efficiency and convenience over nature and natural challenge. Our chronic disconnection from outdoor adventure means we're underestimating its benefits for our wellbeing. We think of adventure as a luxury, not a necessity, and by doing so, have lost the understanding of how good it makes us feel and how transformative its power can be. Ignoring the call to adventure has become the status quo.

Thanks to advances in technology and improvements in housing standards we go outdoors less than any generation before us. We are safer and more comfortable than ever before. Standards of living are better for the vast majority of us than they have ever been. And yet, for the first time since records began, life expectancy has fallen in several developed countries in recent years and mental-health problems have reached an all-time high. In an age of such wealth and comfort, this seems paradoxical. Living sedentary, unadventurous lives affects our physical and mental health, making us unfit, more anxious and less resilient.

The biggest change has been in the last thirty years. My friend Richie (who you will meet later in the book swimming the rapids of the mighty Zambezi River) noted that when he was at school, he'd play in the woodland behind the playground every break time, free and unsupervised. His son now goes to the same school and the woodland is still there. However, today it is fenced off, surrounded by warning signs, and no one is allowed to enter unless it's during weekly structured forest-school lessons. This is the new normal.

In short, modern life, for too many of us, has become too restrictive. We've become victims of convenience – bored, risk averse and disconnected from the natural world. Beyond making us unwell, the absence of adventure is keeping us from being the best versions of ourselves that we can be. But there is another way. Taking my two decades of experience as an adventurer and the latest research in brain and behaviour, I'll show you the many positive effects adventure can have for individuals, groups and society, and how a more adventurous life enables us:

- To heal, recover and rise after adversity
- To bring up well-rounded and resilient children
- To face fear
- To stretch ourselves and grow
- To strengthen relationships
- To find joy
- To find meaning
- To boost wellbeing and life satisfaction
- To optimise how we function on a day-to-day basis (how we think, feel and behave)
- To become our best selves

In the first three chapters, we'll explore the impact adventure has on people and what poets and philosophers have known for eons: that adventure matters. We will also address what happens when we lack adventure in our lives and what we can do about it. Then, in chapter four and beyond, we'll delve more deeply into the specific ways adventure can help us become our best selves, and we'll uncover the surprisingly simple ways that you can live more adventurously without the need to quit your job and cycle round the world or throw yourself off a bungee jump.

I truly believe that adventure is a necessity for our wellbeing, physically and mentally. It teaches us to confront challenges, to take risks, and to appreciate our wild places and each other – all while giving us moments of real joy. What's more, anyone can do it.

And it's fun. There are so many things we're told we should be doing to make ourselves happier and healthier: going to the gym, cutting out sugar, reducing the salt we eat, going to therapy, being mindful. It can be exhausting just thinking about everything we ought to be doing. But the beauty of adventure is that it's natural and fun (even when it's not fun; more about that in chapter nine). Adventure is something to look forward to, a pleasure to look back on and mostly enjoyable at the time too. As such, adventure is a welcome addition to our list of 'must dos' as we strive to be healthier and happier.

At the end of the day, adventure might just be the most natural way to make a change and tackle the many health issues that we face. I hope *Adventure Revolution* will help spark a change for you, the reader, and maybe even in society more widely. Let it tempt you to get up, go outside and try something new.

One

Inspiration Contagion

'Not because it is easy, but because it is hard.'

John F. Kennedy

Two thousand feet up the side of Concepción, an active volcano in central Nicaragua, the mud-spattered wheelchair lay on its side, its green frame glinting in the unforgiving sun, the metal too hot to touch. Climbing karabiners and straps lay abandoned around it; a coil of rope hung off the seat. Not surprisingly, given its extraordinary location, this was no ordinary wheelchair. It had four equal-sized wheels with thick tyres to navigate the rock-strewn terrain, wide handlebars at the back for pushing and brakes at the front for the user to control the speed. This beaten-up piece of equipment looked like it had been somewhere and meant something. And it had: it was currently twenty-seven days into a coast-to-coast crossing of Nicaragua. The clinking of karabiners against the frame, the creaking of rope under tension and the audible straining of human breath no longer surrounded it. Now, in the hot still air, there was only silence.

The chair had been abandoned by Ade Adepitan, who had lost the use of his legs to polio as a child and had become Britain's best-known wheelchair basketball player. After winning a bronze medal at the 2004 Paralympics, he and his mane of long locks had regularly appeared on TV. And now, his wheelchair defeated, he was half the way up the volcano on his hands and knees, making a bid for the summit with Karl, a one-legged amputee he'd met just weeks before.

I have only to gaze into the distance for all the years to drop away, and I see them again, these two men struggling upwards together. I have many adventure tales to tell, but this became one of the most important expeditions I'd ever participate in. For it wasn't just *my* life touched for ever by these five weeks in Central America; the journey had a profound impact on the whole team – novices and experienced adventurers alike – but also, crucially, on everyone who witnessed it.

In late 2004, several months before we faced the volcano, I had been invited to join the expedition, named *Beyond Boundaries*. Expedition leader Ken Hames, an ex-major in the SAS, was planning to lead eleven people across Nicaragua from the Atlantic coast to the Pacific Ocean, a 220-mile crossing. The entire expedition was to be televised on prime-time BBC TV. However, not only did the selected explorers have zero expedition experience, they were also physically disabled. The team included two wheelchair users, Ade and Sophie; Jane, who had lost both her lower legs; and Karl, Lorraine and Glenn, each of whom had one leg. Then there were Warren and Toby, each with one arm; Daryl with spina bifida; Amar, who was blind; and Charlie, who was deaf.

By the time we reached the volcano, several team members had dropped out for different reasons. Those remaining had crossed hundreds of miles of thick jungle and dry savannah. The physical effort of pushing wheelchairs through sticky mud and clambering through uneven terrain would be difficult for anyone. But in doing so without being able to see or hear, and with extraordinary strain on muscles, tendons, prosthetic legs and arms, the remaining team members had already overcome what had seemed impossible.

Yet summiting the volcano would prove to be the toughest challenge yet. From its base, the volcano filled the entire sky, obliterating the landscape all around; its sides rose ominously above us and stretched in every direction, overwhelmingly everywhere. The team rigged the wheelchair to straps and pullies so it could be manhandled up the slope by a three-man team and held from rolling backwards after each push. The hauling team of Karl, Toby and Amar worked together to help Ade push his wheelchair nearly halfway up the volcano. That in itself was a seemingly insurmountable challenge. However, the already treacherous rocky terrain suddenly changed from a thirty-degree to forty-five-degree incline. Over the next two exhausting hours, the team covered just 600 feet. The incline had become too steep; the painfully slow progress was just too much to bear. They reluctantly agreed it wouldn't be possible to take the wheelchair any further. Ade needed to find another way to reach the summit.

It was too much. He broke down and cried. Ade is so strong I couldn't bear to watch this happen – none of us could. It was soul destroying, and yet completely and utterly human. I cried for the first time on that expedition too. It was the only time I'd witnessed Ade to be anything but determined to get to the top. Seeing his face show a hint of defeat knocked the whole team for six. Ade had been the driving force and morale booster of the team throughout the entire expedition due to his unstoppable, positive energy. Nothing had dented his ability to dig deep and find more reserves, until now.

And for Ade, this was vulnerability in the extreme. Televised. But he resolved to keep going. He crawled and hauled himself upwards. Inch by inch, with either his thighs or knees scraping painfully over the burning-hot volcanic rock, Ade dragged himself up that volcano with all his might. To ease the pain, he'd swap between two positions: pushing himself up with his arms in an outward sitting position and crawling on his hands and knees. Karl remained by his side for every push, drag and strain.

Five excruciating hours later, they reached the summit. A completely shattered Ade lay on the ground and, gripping onto Karl's hand, quietly wept. 'Karl, man,' he said. 'Thanks, man. That's the hardest thing I've ever done, full stop. Without a doubt!' He'd reached the summit by crawling and pulling himself up more than 3,000 feet without the aid and security of his chair.

Ade explained to me in 2020, sixteen years after the summit, that he'd returned from his 'seismic challenge' of an adventure for ever changed. He recalled how he'd felt at the time of abandoning his wheelchair: 'My heart sunk as I thought, What am I going to do here? I always saw getting into a chair as a way of getting from A to B in a more digni-fied manner, a way of keeping my self-respect. I had a flash-back to when I was called "black monkey" because of the way I had to crawl around. My wheelchair gave me a chance to do so many things; it was like discovering the greatest invention in the world. It has been my biggest source of empowerment. So, getting out of it on the volcano meant I had to deal with ideas of lost independence, all captured on camera and shown to the world.'

When I asked him how he felt about it now, he had a different outlook: 'The way I looked, I thought people would see me as weaker if I showed vulnerability, but now I see that it's a strength to show it, and I worry less about how others perceive me.' Even after all this time, he saw that relatively brief period in his life as a major turning point, which he still thought about every couple of weeks, calling it his 'watershed – a life affirming point' when he realised what was possible. 'My life is split into before and after *Beyond Boundaries*. Challenging and achieving the impossible is something I'm used to talking about and dealing with as an athlete, but when you do something you didn't think you could do – *that* is special! That empowers you, supercharges you, cements who you are and what you should be trying to achieve.'

Ade explained it was different to sport, because it was out of his comfort zone completely. He was used to the basketball court, having trained all his life and prepared himself for that from age eleven. But he had never prepared himself for the unforeseen challenges of being an adventurer, which, Ade said, freed him.

Adventure opened Ade up to pursue possibilities he'd not have considered before. Fifteen years later, now a household name, Ade's latest TV series *Africa with Ade Adepitan*, showing him discovering Africa by (albeit more conventional) wheelchair, had recently aired, and Ade was bringing his passion for adventure to others and inspiring more people with his charity work.

For me, the way Ade explained his life as split into 'before and after' his adventure conjured up an image of a butterfly. They are of course a symbol of change, but it was also because of the sight that had greeted us when we reached the summit of Concepción. The landscape was barren on the final ascent; we climbed hot, dusty rock with choking sulphurous fumes billowing around us. But as we reached the top, a bright yellow shape flew across my path. Looking up, the air seemed to be alive with shifting colours, the unforgiving parched landscape suddenly transformed by a kaleidoscope of shapes and tones. I remember, as we sat to take it all in, hundreds of butterflies filling the air, brushing our bare skin, occasionally landing to share our seats of rock. The moving current of wings was surreal, otherworldly, amid this human drama, and I remember feeling awestruck by this extraordinary scene and uplifted by the delightful wonder of multicoloured butterflies fluttering all around us. The beauty of it was overwhelming. It was like they were spurring us on and celebrating our achievement and our transformation. In the midst of adventure, even though it had so far been defined by pain and heartache, this moment of magic made us feel deeply alive and grateful to be so. And it was this that defined the experience. But it wasn't until we arrived home that the symbolic serendipity of the butterflies hit home. That expedition took us all through our own version of metamorphosis.

Nobody returned home the same. The enormity of the task and the level of jeopardy had been extreme. The coast-to-coast crossing alone had been a huge undertaking for any team, whether able bodied or differently abled. Miles of thick jungle with few pathways had merged onto endless stretches of baked savannah. Add to that the uncertainty about how different medical conditions would react to the rigorous conditions and climate, and we had literally been walking – or rolling – new ground. Yet it was the incredibly demanding nature of the challenge that had given it such immense power as a catalyst for change.

Every one of us, from the participants to the filming and safety crew, had been pushed so far outside our individual comfort zones. But we'd all noticed, once we'd emerged on the other side, that our sense of what could be achieved had changed. After accomplishing more than we thought we could, that's when we saw ourselves and the world afresh, with a renewed perspective about our own capabilities. It was extremely powerful. Indeed, how we all felt about ourselves and our sense of accomplishment was more deeply experienced than any of us had expected, like nothing any of us had ever known before.

This was partly because we had an audience, the biggest of which was back home in the UK, six months after the trip, when millions tuned in to watch four one-hour episodes documenting the epic journey on BBC Two. The other audience was made up of the people of Nicaragua, those in the remote villages we passed through. They couldn't help but be impressed by this menagerie of extraordinary humans who were beating the odds to travel hundreds of miles from coast to coast.

The story of these ordinary people doing something extraordinary resonated with every member of that combined audience, no matter what community or background or country they came from. This story of people with disabilities doing the impossible spoke to a deep part of what it means to be human and how we strive to achieve fulfilling lives.

'It was the original disruptor,' Ade said. 'We flipped the status quo on its head. Everything people knew about what can or can't be done. The last thing anyone expected was differently abled people trekking through the toughest jungle in the world.' The heroes of *Beyond Boundaries* turned disability into inspirational ability. More than that, they had shown the world what was possible. Consequently, the impact reached far beyond the Nicaraguan villages. The power of adventure to expose the self-imposed limitations we set ourselves and reveal that you can *always* do more than you thought when faced with challenges – *that* power was contagious to those watching our televised adventure.

Viewers got to witness each team member's journey from the beginning. After filling in her application form to join the *Beyond Boundaries* expedition, Lorraine had walked to the end of her garden for the first time in six years since losing her leg in a traffic accident. Viewers saw how the mere idea of the adventure had been enough to shift her perception about what she might be capable of. That prospect of what was possible had ignited action in her. When the TV series was aired, showing Lorraine and the rest of the team striving for the impossible, the effect on viewers was immediate.

As friends, colleagues and family members witnessed their loved ones doing something they never thought possible, it greatly impacted how they perceived the world and their own capabilities, creating a ripple effect. And the same was true for the rest of the viewing public. They were experiencing the contagion of adventure: it has the power to not only empower the person who went on the adventure, but also their sister, their friend and their parents, leading us all to question what we are truly capable of. After all, if glamourous indoorsy Lorraine from Accounts can walk across Nicaragua with one leg, what might I be able to do?

By giving this story a television audience, the ripple effect was amplified: the Audience Appreciation Index (AI) is a score out of 100 used to indicate the public's appreciation for a television or radio programme in the United Kingdom. At the BBC an AI of 85 or over is considered excellent, over 90 is exceptional. From memory, *Beyond Boundaries* gained a score of 94, the highest AI figure they could remember.

The effect on the team was profound and moving. But what was more extraordinary was what happened after the first episode aired. Letters started to arrive. Not emails, but actual handwritten letters were sent to the production offices by the sackful. Letters sharing inspirational stories of new beginnings and fresh courage to try new activities poured in from hundreds of disabled and able-bodied viewers, each of them sharing the new steps they were taking and the boundaries they were crossing. From the man who had stood up immediately after the show and walked to his corner shop for the first time since losing his leg in surgery, to the blind man who had been inspired to start a running club for the visually impaired and the teenage girl who'd decided to return to school. Although not physically disabled, she'd suffered from poor confidence, and the show had helped her to put things into perspective, making her realise she had far less to worry about than she'd thought.

A flood of stories arrived from people who had been inspired and encouraged by what they'd seen, people who were standing up and venturing out into an uncertain world, facing challenges head on with a renewed sense of vigour and vitality. One story, about a teenage boy from Leeds, stuck in my memory. His mother had written to tell us that the day after watching *Beyond Boundaries* her son had returned to his football club, a place he'd not been to since losing his arm in a motorcycle accident two years before. In her hand-written letter, she explained this proactive move by her son had demonstrated a fundamental change in how he'd previously been dealing with his new disability and gave them both hope for the future. A door towards new possibilities and fresh beginnings had been opened – a door towards hope.

Having led expeditions for more than a decade, I was expecting this one to have a life-changing impact on some of the team. I had always felt like adventure had saved my life. It had been my therapy, my crucible and my companion, and I'd witnessed the transformational power of adventure many times in others since the Amazon expedition with Alice three years earlier. But I hadn't reckoned on this expedition changing the lives of those watching. Witnessing this audience reaction and reading these remarkable tales of people from all over the country being called to do something which had previously scared them, to embark on their own bold journeys in life, this just added fuel to the fire of my quest to better understand the positive impact of adventure on people.

Evidently, adventure stories inspire us; they allow us to see the hero in ourselves and to expand what we believe is possible. There is something so universal in these tales that it impacts people of all ages, abilities and nationalities. Our televised journey hit a chord somewhere deep down in our collective history. I believe this is because it spoke to something primal within us – that being adventurous is an innate part of being human. In sharing adventure stories – both fact and fiction – we can speak directly to this ancient part of each of us, the inner adventurers sitting behind our desks, snuggling on our sofas or stuck in a traffic jam, who yearn for untamed adventure and the opportunity to prove what we can do and uncover who we are. Seeing others rising to triumph over great adversity empowers us all to face head on whatever we might encounter.

A story as old as the human race

'Why do you go away? So that you can come back. So that you can see the place you came from with new eyes and extra colours. And the people there see you differently, too. Coming back to where you started is not the same as never leaving.'

Terry Pratchett

Since the beginning of the human race, we've been telling stories. As far back as history, myth or memory can go, there is one story that endures and is as relevant today as it was to our hunter-gatherer ancestors – the story of the call to adventure. Our oral and written history is peppered with stories of scaling mountains and crossing oceans; symbols of high adventure, exploration and transformation are scattered throughout literature. This timeless narrative of adventure features across numerous cultures, from tribal stories untouched by the modern world to those featured in modern entertainment. Such is its importance that this calling has been the topic of research for many years and now has a name to describe it: the hero's journey. A tale about a would-be hero who starts in the ordinary world, is called to adventure and completes a series of challenges. After rising to meet those challenges, the once ordinary person returns home, changed, now a hero. In modern times, it has been analysed and popularised by Joseph Campbell, who devoted his life to studying worldwide myths. It was Campbell who gave it a formula and first called it the hero's journey, an archetype that appears everywhere from *The Odyssey* to *Star Wars* and beyond. All of the stories featuring the hero's journey share the same elements and follow a number of steps along the journey:

1. **Ordinary world** – The hero's journey begins in the ordinary world, the place where the hero lives his life before this journey begins.
2. **Call to adventure** – The hero must leave the safety of the ordinary world, to undertake a quest involving challenges, when he receives a call to adventure. First, he will need to overcome fears about embarking on the quest. As a reader or viewer, we tend to share the hero's fears about venturing into the unknown, but while there is risk, the promise of reward for heeding the call to adventure will be far greater and is ultimately necessary.
3. **Meeting the mentor** – The hero may need some guidance in the form of training, advice, valuable

insight or object, and, perhaps, something to help him boost his own self-confidence. In this way, the mentor provides something that helps the hero to overcome his fears and become sufficiently brave to continue.

4. **Crossing the threshold** – Armed with this renewed strength or wisdom, the hero commits to heed the call to adventure and crosses the threshold from the ordinary world into an unknown world where familiar rules do not apply.

5. **The road of trials** – Now the hero has stepped outside of his comfort zone, he'll embark on a road of trials and face a number of challenges and obstacles that he must rise to and overcome. As the hero rises to each challenge, we gain further insight into who they are as a person.

6. **The inmost cave** – This is where the hero must prepare himself ahead of facing the ultimate test. The cave could be a location, or it could represent inner conflict that the hero needs to work through before going forward.

7. **The supreme ordeal** – This is where the hero faces the greatest challenge and biggest hardship of their journey. He'll need to use all of the skills and strengths he's gained during the journey thus far in order to survive.

8. **Reward and transformation** – Having successfully risen to the challenge and endured the ordeal, the hero receives a reward. Part of this reward is the transformation of the hero into a better version of himself, through the application of new knowledge, insight or self-awareness.

9. **The road back home** – The hero can now make his journey home, feeling a great sense of achievement and pride.

10. **Returning with the reward** – In this final stage of the journey, the hero returns home, for ever changed, to his ordinary world. He has faced hardship and risen to challenges, and as a result he has grown. He brings new hope and will use his reward to improve his ordinary world and make his life and the lives of those living in the ordinary world better. This is what Campbell calls the 'application of the boon'.

The hero's journey is used as a model in fiction writing, but it is a reflection of real life, of real adventure, which has originated from shared human history. Audiences of the *Beyond Boundaries* programme saw the team at the start of their journey in the 'ordinary world', witnessing their vulnerabilities, and then travelled with them on their quest to Nicaragua. They saw our heroes stepping out of their comfort zones, embarking on a 'road of trials' from the Atlantic coast to the Pacific Ocean. Some didn't make it to the end. Others faced the 'inmost cave', leapt into the unknown and conquered their fears. Ade's summit of the volcano was his 'supreme ordeal', where he drew on every ounce of his strength to make it through. As a result, he was rewarded and transformed. He, along with the rest of the team, became the best version of himself and took the 'road back home' glowing with pride, for ever changed and emboldened as a result of his adventure.

'Ordinary' life is improved by the treasure (and transformation) you bring back into it. This holds true for every adventure I've been on. And this is why this book is filled with hero's journey stories that reveal the types of transformation that people discover as a result of adventuring. It is precisely this part – of bringing treasured skills, knowledge, strength and transformation from adventure back into ordinary life – that is so important. Adventure allows us to shift perspectives and change who we are and how we respond to whatever crosses our paths during our life's journeys, to rewrite our own stories and ultimately to create our happy endings. Encouraging ourselves to physically embark on adventurous activities is a key part of the Adventure Revolution, but so too is adapting our inbuilt storytelling machines (our minds) to be bold and discover more about ourselves and what we're truly capable of. When we think of ourselves as adventurers embarking on the journey of life and navigating around the obstacles in our paths, it empowers us to take on those inevitable challenges and become our own heroes.

We're not just inspired by adventure stories for their transformational effect at an individual level. Being witness to an epic adventure can also prove to us what our institutions, communities and nations are able to achieve, broadening our imaginations to what is possible. This can spark hope not just for a 'better me' but for a better world.

Human possibility

Stories of archetypal heroes' adventures have long been a source of national pride. One of the most iconic moments of adventurous endeavour in human history, the summitting of Mount Everest by Edmund Hillary and Tenzing Norgay, gave postwar Britain much needed hope. The success of the British-led expedition (headed by Colonel John Hunt) was announced on the day Queen Elizabeth II was crowned, 2 June 1953. The combination of a new monarch and the success of a British-led team being the first to reach the top of the world signalled a new era and significantly buoyed a nation weary of war and postwar hardship. It fuelled hope that Britain could rebuild and rise to a bright future, and maybe even suggested that that future had already begun.

Similarly, on 20 July 1969, the *Apollo 11* mission inspired a generation; however, this time the whole world was watching. President John F. Kennedy's dream of putting a man on the moon seemed a waste of national resources to some, during a time otherwise dominated by the conflict in Vietnam and the Cold War. Yet, fifty years later it is still an enduring symbol of human achievement, a rallying call for what's possible. That first moon landing united the world, albeit only briefly. Six hundred million people across the globe watched the moment on television as Neil Armstrong took that small step for man and giant leap for humanity. Awestruck viewers saw images of Earth rising on the moon's horizon. Every person witnessing that step, that leap, had been given, quite literally, a new perspective of the world and of what mankind is capable of. In this way, adventure not only celebrates human endeavour, it also communicates human possibility.

Today, the possibilities painted by the adventurers we read and hear about continue to inspire us to consider what we might be able to achieve and even give us hope for a better society. The combination of the two is life changing, maybe even world changing. If you're personally empowered and you're given the glimpse of a better world, then you can take action and maybe make the impossible possible.

The *Beyond Boundaries* experience and two of the most iconic adventure moments of the twentieth century demonstrate the far-reaching and enduring power of adventure. These might appear isolated and extreme examples of transformation; however, in my two decades of leading expeditions, I have seen this change in almost everyone who has undertaken an adventure. You don't have to climb a volcano or step on the moon to inspire those around you. Ordinary people take on extraordinary adventures every day. Whether you're cycling city to city, camping in the wilderness or learning to kayak for the first time, you will inspire your friends, your children and your colleagues to face their fears and join in too. We are most inspired by those closest to us, by those who start in the same place, the same 'ordinary world', but who still venture forth to answer a call to adventure. By sharing our adventures and our transformations (however insignificant we might think they are) we can ignite a spark in others, create an inspiration contagion and eventually an 'Adventure Revolution'.

Two

Why Adventure Matters

'The wonderful things in life are the things you do, not the things you have.'

Reinhold Messner, mountaineer

The body of research demonstrating that physical and psychological wellbeing can benefit from exposure to nature is now very substantial. The 'nature effect' is rightly recognised as an important factor in our health, and it is often cited as the main or only reason quoted for the positive impact of outdoor activity on our wellbeing. However, I'd argue there is a vital element, that of adventure, that is as important and works in unison with nature. Let's look at the evidence for both.

Forest bathing, for example, in which people deliberately immerse themselves in the natural world, has grown in popularity across the world because we now know that spending time in nature improves mental and physical wellbeing. In 2018, researchers from the University of East Anglia analysed 143 earlier studies and found that exposure to green space reduced blood pressure, the stress hormone cortisol and the risk of diabetes, as well as helping us to live longer. A Japanese study published in the *Environmental Health and Preventive Medicine* journal in 2010 found that the essential oils, phytoncides, that trees release into the air bolster our immune system by increasing the activity of our natural killer cells to control infections and tumour growth. And a bacteria found in soil, *Mycobacterium vaccae*, has been proven to bolster our resilience against stress, so much so that a team of scientists from the University of Colorado are calling it a potential 'stress vaccine'. Further evidence suggests that spending time in nature activates our parasympathetic nervous system that triggers our 'rest and digest' response. This essentially means we feel reassured, relaxed and safe after exposure to it. Our nervous system balances out.

Evidently, spending time in nature makes us feel better. It can even make us better people. A series of studies were published in 2009 under the title 'Can Nature Make Us More Caring? Effects of Immersion in Nature on Intrinsic Aspirations and Generosity'. The researchers found that exposure to nature can make us nicer to others by fostering values that relate to building relationships and community. The study measured what the participants valued in life: wealth and fame ('to be financially successful' and 'to be admired by many people') and connectedness and community ('to have deep enduring relationships' and 'to work toward the betterment of society'). Participants who were immersed in natural environments rated close relationships and community higher than they had previously. In contrast, those exposed to man-made elements valued wealth and fame higher than before the immersion. The researchers also found that those who had been immersed in nature behaved more generously than those in the urban environments. Overall, these results suggest that nature brings individuals closer, whereas human-made environments orient goals toward more selfish ends. It's hard not to be inspired by the possibilities: imagine if we could get our world leaders to spend a bit more time out in nature.

In 1984, Harvard University biologist Edward O. Wilson first coined the phrase 'biophilia' to describe the idea that humans have 'ingrained' in our genes an instinctive bond with nature and the living organisms we cohabit with. It's taken decades, but, thankfully, the nature effect has become more widely known, accepted and acted upon in recent years. Nature is now routinely prescribed by doctors for physical and mental rehabilitation.

It's important to acknowledge the benefits that sport and travel have on wellbeing too, including the natural highs experienced during exercise, the sustained reward of feeling fitter, and the capacity of travel to both broaden the mind and to help us appreciate what we already have. These, like nature, are well documented and powerful elements of most, if not all, adventurous activities.

However, it's the element of adventure itself – a mix of challenge, adversity and uncertainty – that is generally overlooked when we consider wellbeing. It's the difference between taking some exercise, or spending time in nature passively soaking up the benefits, and being immersed in an exciting outdoor challenge. Adventure is the ingredient that marks the difference between tennis and climbing, swimming and wild swimming, forest bathing and exploring your local woodland. As an activity that we can take part in outdoors, adventure can enable wellbeing in even more ways than nature or sport on their own (or even combined). It's time to acknowledge adventure as part of the solution to peak physical and mental health. At the same time, we need to remove the mystique and remind ourselves that adventure can be on any scale; whether you're camping out for the first time or you're participating in free solo (without ropes) climbing, like nature and exercise, it can be accessible to everyone.

The multitude of ways adventure can transform is why it excites me so much. Not just the act of adventuring itself, but what it can do for us as human beings navigating our way through the ups and downs of life. This is what I call the 'Adventure Effect', which lays on a spectrum between deep and permanent transformational change to a less extreme but still impactful shift towards feeling better than before and thinking with a fresh perspective and more helpful mindset. It's possible to transform your life – how you think, how you feel and what you do – with one simple intention: to live more adventurously.

This was the case for Kelvyn James. We first spoke in 2019, and I was so moved by Kelvyn's experience and the impact the Adventure Effect had had on his life that I felt compelled to help him share his story. The following year, when I launched Adventure Mind, the first ever conference to focus on the impact of adventure on wellbeing, to nearly 200 international researchers and practitioners, Kelyvn was there to tell his story.

During his early childhood, Kelvyn had a violently abusive stepfather and found his only escape came during the adventures he'd go on with his inner-city scouting group. This became his safe place: 'I loved that group, because we'd camp and make fires, and it helped me to survive that time.' Back then, adventure was an escape: 'I thought I was just having a good time, making friends, laughing a lot, surviving the odd close call.' But little did Kelvyn know that it would someday become a lifeline and a legacy.

Kelvyn's early taste of adventure with the Scouts led him into rock climbing, which he immersed himself in from the age of seventeen. Climbing gave him the opportunity to forget what was happening at home and focus on the moment. As such, Kelvyn's early teens and twenties were filled with adventure.

However, a decade later, Kelvyn had gone off track. He had established a successful commercial glazing business, and he owned flash cars and a big house, but long hours managing forty-eight employees gradually replaced the climbing, as did the beginning of a drinking problem. 'Climbing was squeezed out and adventure disappeared from my life,' Kelvyn said. 'I went from a nine-stone climber to a fifteen-stone drinker before I finally sold the business.'

The decision to sell up came after the unthinkable happened. In 2010, Kelvyn's mother was murdered by her third husband. Lost in grief, Kelvyn needed to find a way to prevent himself and his family from breaking apart. Together, they endured the ordeal of a murder trial and further appeals. This resulted in an unimaginable five years of litigation with his mother's killer that was so harrowing Kelvyn's barrister took early retirement at its conclusion. During the incomprehensible pain of the trial, Kelvyn sold the business as it dawned on him that money and success weren't what mattered most. His drinking could have developed into a real problem. Instead, having not climbed for almost a decade, he returned to hard running and extreme climbing.

'At first, I just needed a distraction from the grief,' Kelvyn said. 'I didn't want to be around people, so I went and climbed some big ridges on my own. Living in the moment stopped me staring into the abyss.' Kelvyn thought that it was the mindful experience of becoming lost in the moment that helped him to avoid getting lost in despair. Those formative years in the Scouts sowed the seed of climbing as a critical coping mechanism, something he could return to when he needed it the most.

Kelvyn attributed his adventure background as being the source of his ability to survive: 'I could keep going, because mountaineering had made me resilient.' In his experience, rising to extreme climbs gave him a sense of resilience and capability that proved to himself that he could survive adversity: 'Knowing you can deal with this, whatever it is, gives you the strength to carry on when the way ahead seems lost, when you quite literally have to walk out of the dark.'

Those challenging climbs also restored Kelvyn's faith in humanity: 'Those adventures, they taught me to trust in the good of others. When I came face to face with the very worst that people could be, when it looked like I might break, I had friends ready to catch me, to support me, to tell me I could and would carry on.'

Adventure had given Kelvyn the gift of resilience, trust and hope. And when his friends took him to do the Tour de Mont Blanc hiking route, it gave him another gift: a bright future. The trip inspired Kelvyn to do a mountain-leadership course, and he soon realised how much he thrived when taking people on adventures. Now he rarely climbs and considers himself more of a 'trekker'. He has progressed from extreme climbing, as a way to distract himself, to the joy of helping others to do things that are new to them. (This is extraordinarily similar to my own experience and how I feel about adventure today. I wonder how many other adventure instructors and guides feel that their 'job' is more their 'calling'?) 'The look on their faces as they made those discoveries was priceless,' said Kelvyn, who soon realised that it was through giving people the gift of adventure and 'making memories for others' that he could find what he needed. 'It was the giving part that gave me calm and peace,' explained Kelvyn. 'Climbing E9 didn't do that, but other people's reactions did. It made me my best me, and it's something that would've made my mum proud.'

Kelvyn now spends half his time working as a mental-health professional for Mental Health Northwest and the other half as an outdoor leader in the mountains taking people on 'Wellness Walks'. 'It's the ten-year anniversary of losing my mother,' Kelvyn told me at my 2020 Adventure Mind conference. 'It seems a lifetime ago. Now, I'm as rounded and well balanced as a human can be thanks to my return to adventure. I genuinely speak to my mum more now than I ever did. When I am in the mountains, I am in touch with her somehow, because I am being my best me, and it has nothing to do with the trappings of life. I did "rich", and it didn't make me happy. Now I'm doing "happy", and I feel truly rich. This me knows there's something more, knows there's beauty in the world; this me is my best me.'

★   ★   ★

While I've seen the transformational power of adventure up close and personal, both in myself and many others, the evidence for its benefits is far more than anecdotal. There is a growing body of research to support the idea that adventure has positive effects on overall wellbeing. According to one sports medicine study, titled 'Adventurous Physical Activity Environments as a Mainstream Intervention for Mental Health', individuals taking part in adventure report a huge number of positive transformations, among them: increased quality of and engagement with life; improved emotional regulation; enhanced social connection; improved goal achievement; improved joy. Similarly, positive results have been found across decades of adventure education and adventure-therapy programmes, including managing anxiety and overcoming fear, finding self-worth and building inter-personal connections, resulting in participants becoming happier, healthier and more confident.

In November 2017, researcher Hetty Key from Women in Adventure asked me to help her to contact subjects through the adventure community I'd founded, Explorers Connect, for a new study. She interviewed more than 2,000 women, 99.6 per cent of whom agreed or strongly agreed that outdoor adventure had a positive impact on their mental wellbeing, along with their physical wellbeing, resilience, self-esteem and future outlook. The results from two pilot studies published in the *Journal of Adolescence* in 2016 showed that teenage team members reported an increase in life satisfaction after a nine-day hike through the Alps, and adult participants that took part in an eight-day wilderness adventure in the Norwegian Hardangervidda region scored higher in life satisfaction and happiness and lower in stress following the experience.

As I've discovered during my own work in this field, the positive effect caused by adventure isn't just temporary. Researcher John Hattie states in his 1997 report, which analysed ninety-six adventure-education studies, that 'it seems that adventure programs have a major impact on the lives of participants, and this impact is lasting'. The evidence for the positive difference adventure makes to people's lives is finally being more widely recognised, and doctors and other health professionals are increasingly offering adventure as a therapy.

Adventure has always played a critical role in human development, but many of us have become separated from adventure in our everyday lives. This shift from unavoidable to primarily recreational happened only relatively recently. In order to experience adventure today, we need to seek out an activity that is away from our normal, comfortable indoor lives. But first, to understand and reintroduce it into our day-to-day experiences, we'll need to identify what adventure is.

Although there's no agreed definition amongst researchers, one of the more established explanations describes adventure as 'a variety of self-initiated activities and experiences, usually utilising a close interaction with the natural environment, that contain elements of real or apparent risk, in which the outcome is uncertain but can be influenced by participant and/or circumstance'. And in the 2020 study 'Health and Wellbeing in an Outdoor and Adventure Sports Context', the authors identified unique aspects of adventure activities, such as discomfort and physical challenge, that cannot be replicated by other activities (such as traditional sports) and are directly linked to improved wellbeing.

When I think of adventure, especially in the context of wellbeing today, it's a voluntary activity with three essential elements: challenge, uncertainty and adversity. If we look at each of these three elements in turn, we can get a closer understanding of what 'adventure' entails.

A challenge is a task or situation that tests someone's abilities. It can take place in the most inhospitable terrain, from scaling the highest mountain and kayaking through the wildest waters to crossing deserts in the hottest conditions – the kind of well-outside-your-comfort-zone adventure that tests your mental and physical abilities as you strive to reach the most extreme peak, pole or shore. This acute end of adventure can include multiday expeditions or extreme sports, like BASE jumping, that are experienced in just minutes. Many of the stories shared across these pages relate to this kind of great, big, challenging adventure. However, some of the stories relate to smaller yet equally transformational types of adventure too. The smaller kind of challenge involves choosing to follow smaller pockets of excitement, which still play at the edges of your comfort zone but fit into your weekend, evening or lunch break. It could be a ten-minute break from the routine where you engage in parkour, climb a tree or explore a new area around your home or office; it could be an evening or weekend away in nature to enjoy the thrill of successfully lighting your own campfire, climbing a hill to watch the sunrise or sleeping out under the stars. Adventure involves challenge, whether big or small, in your garden or far from home.

The most exciting challenges are those that involve uncertainty, where there are no guarantees or binary outcomes. Without uncertainty, we have a familiar and predictable experience; we don't have adventure. Adventurers choose to go into the unknown; for me, it's the difference between jogging the same circuit around town or pioneering new routes every time I leave the house. Choosing to step into the unknown is psychologically uncomfortable: you will feel anxious, even afraid, because you are missing information. But you have a choice: you can continue to crave certainty, or you can start to recognise that it's the uncertainty that is fuelling your engagement, and this is where learning and growth happen.

If you don't at some point feel uncomfortable, cold, hot, tired or scared, it's not an adventure. Adversity is an important part of adventuring, because it signals to us that we are pushing ourselves, overcoming physical or psychological obstacles. Explorers choose to go on adventures despite knowing there will be difficulties to bear because they know there is a greater payoff in the end. The taste of success is sweeter when you've sacrificed along the journey. The way in which we can change our response to adversity is another key benefit of participating in adventure that you can take back to everyday life. Society is driving us to strive to be comfortable above all else, but this isn't our natural state – it turns out adversity is actually good for us. A 2010 study published in the *Journal of Personality and Social Psychology* assessed 2,398 participants and found that people who had experienced some lifetime adversity reported better mental health and wellbeing not only than those with a history of frequent adversity, but also of subjects who had experienced no difficulties in life. The researchers suggest that 'in moderation, whatever does not kill us may indeed make us stronger'.

There is evidence to show that taking part in voluntary activities that contain elements of challenge, uncertainty and adversity help our wellbeing. Both to help people to recover from mental illness but also to encourage anyone to be the best that they can be, to live their best life. Indeed, adventure can help us to feel, think and do better. And this trilogy is of crucial importance, because it's these three elements – our thoughts, our feelings and our actions – that are mostly responsible for determining our level of wellbeing.

Think better

After returning from an adventure, many people report feeling a calm acceptance and ability to put everyday struggles into perspective. For example, many responses to the Women in Adventure survey noted the calming effect of adventurous activities. 'It calms my mind and allows me to de-stress from chaotic technology focused days,' said one. 'It helps me look at the whole picture and realise one small problem is only a hurdle along the way,' said another.

Personally, I've found I don't get flustered by things outside of my control or dwell on stuff like my pre-adventure self did. Perhaps this ability to put things into perspective and see things we might have been struggling with in a different light comes as a result of coping with uncertainty and hardship during adventures. Certainly, adventure makes you realise you have what it takes to cope with whatever life throws your way. And adventure has had a profound effect on how I personally deal with uncertainty. I've become far more comfortable not knowing what is around the corner and realise I don't need all the answers to start a project or adventure. These days, rather than fret about the future or fear failure, I know I can face whatever life has in store for me because, through getting on and taking action, no matter what, I will learn something, and I will cope.

Of course, we all have an inner critic that can sabotage our belief in ourselves. But adventure seems to help quiet that internal judge as we boost our self-efficacy and prove to ourselves we are more capable than we thought. Indeed, #MoreThanYouThink is the hashtag of the Outward Bound Trust, an organisation whose blend of authentic adventure in the natural environment along with deliberate learning and a residential experience has been making a positive difference to young people's lives for the past eighty years. Outward Bound repeatedly shows young people they can achieve more than they thought and face challenges they didn't think they could, by drawing on strengths they didn't know they had. Ultimately, when we think better, we feel better and we do better. Each feeds the other.

Feel better

In this social-media-influenced world, which makes us constantly feel like we're not good enough, belief in our strengths and confidence in our abilities is a rebellious act, and an incredibly healthy one. Adventure serves to counter this modern-day culture of comparison. According to an independent evaluation of vulnerable young people in Cornwall between 2013 to 2017, those who participated in a six-week surf-therapy course reported feeling that their confidence, self-esteem and wellbeing had vastly improved. Parents and referrers also noticed a marked increase in young people's positive attitudes. As one participant of the Women in Adventure survey reported, 'Adventure has given me the confidence to be myself and live in the present.' Another female adventurer said, 'Being active outdoors has given me self-esteem, a sense of self-worth and confidence like nothing else ever has.' And, perhaps the most evident of a mental shift towards the positive, another said, 'I now respect what I can do instead of chastising myself for what I'm not.'

Of course, it's more than mastering a kayak roll or nailing a red run on the ski slopes that boosts self-efficacy. While mastery of new skills offers a great sense of achievement, it's noticing our capacity to rise to challenges and overcome difficult situations we'd never have thought possible that impacts how we see ourselves post-adventure. Such shifts in how we think and feel can have a profound and long-lasting effect on how we show up in the world. I know this at first hand.

As a teenager, I didn't feel I was good enough; I was too fat, too ugly, too unpopular, never doing well enough in the classroom or on the sports field. I remember that setbacks would lead me to moments of complete despair. My low self-esteem was the result of having suffered from episodes of violent abuse. Physical abuse is terrifying to experience, but it's the lingering mental torture that is worse. To live day to day with the threat of violence is nerve-shattering. It changes the way you think, the way you do everything. And then of course there's the shame. You begin to believe it is happening to you because you deserve it and no one is helping you because you are not worth it. So, at times, I felt worthless.

A turning point for me was joining the Duke of Edinburgh's Award scheme at my school when I was sixteen years old. It was the expedition part of the programme that held most appeal, a call to adventure. I had not had the opportunity to do anything like it since my early childhood, so I signed up with three of my friends. Rachel, Sian, Owen and I, teenagers more used to the city, carried overloaded backpacks around the Brecon Beacons National Park in Wales. Hiking and camping largely away from adult supervision, the expedition was designed to foster autonomy in our small team.

I loved it. I heard myself taking control, deciding which way we should go, where we'd have lunch and how we'd camp. Charging off ahead, running back to help others, throwing myself into it. I felt confident enough to fully engage, to make decisions, to even take the lead. I was in my element. And it was obvious to others too. It was only a few years ago that my friend Owen commented that during that expedition 'it was like a light came on in you'. Today, with the benefit of hindsight, I realise that Alice and I must have shared these moments of realisation in some way, a decade apart.

Previously, I'd fallen into a pattern of writing off any success I'd had by attributing it to luck or the work of others, missing any chance to build my self-esteem. But there is something indisputable about reaching the summit of a hill or completing a journey on foot. To get there you must engage 100 per cent; you can't just go through the motions. Even if you've had help, from guides or leaders, you've still had to put one foot in front of the other, no matter the weather, your mood or the weight on your back, so you *own* the accomplishment. The physical and mental commitment is unavoidable in adventurous activity, so the outcome is a feeling of true achievement – a feeling that cannot be taken, or given, away. You see the world differently from the top of a mountain, but you also feel differently too. It was only a few days in the wilderness, but I felt a sense of freedom and escape. What I realise now is that it gave me hope and allowed me to believe in myself and my abilities.

I organised several more camping trips during my last two years at school, including the next Duke of Edinburgh's Award expedition. I felt a little bit less of an outsider in those final years. I even gained much better results academically than anyone had expected me to. And these short hiking trips subsequently gave me the courage to go on an even bigger adventure when I left school. Thriving on my first micro-expeditions in the British countryside and subsequently surviving my first big adventure aged eighteen truly empowered me. It gave me evidence to support the possibility that I might be worthwhile. I began to believe in myself and feel better about who I was and what I might be capable of in the future.

Adventure changed me from a victim with low self-esteem to an empowered and confident woman. It took me from feeling worthless and hopeless to feeling able and hopeful. Once I believed I was capable of a bright future, I could start to dream and then to act. Rather than writing off opportunities as out of my reach, I started to think about what I wanted from life – because I deserved to have aspirations, everyone deserves to. I actively started to plan my route to a future I wanted, looking at universities, jobs and adventures, even though others around me, like some teachers, family members and even some friends, thought they were beyond my capabilities. Adventure ultimately offered me hope and possibility.

Adventure also taught me to see opportunities where

others might see threats; it taught me to risk failure and follow my dreams instead of opting for the easy path that was less scary but ultimately limiting, inward looking, oppressive – a path that makes you smaller and smaller over time. It made life more exciting, wherever I was, not just during adventure but post adventure too. And, above all, it made me feel better about who I was. And that is why I'm writing this book. Today, I barely recognise that desperate teenage girl as me. I've rewritten my story, because adventure has given me the confidence to do so. Certainly, the sixteen-year-old version of myself would never have believed I could launch an adventure community and a conference series, become my own boss, that I would regularly speak in public or would travel to eighty-plus countries, working in most of them and achieving a Guinness World Record.

Do better

Feeling more confident about our own capabilities not only helps us to feel better about ourselves – it also helps and motivates us to *do* better. Indeed, defying limitations unlocks our potential to achieve more and to cope with more. Participants in adventure programmes develop the mental strength needed to handle setbacks and to work towards accomplishments. As such, they develop resilience to help them respond better to challenging situations and the capacity to achieve their aspirations. Adventure helps people to cope better with the present and think optimistically about the future.

Adventure also helps people to behave better. For example, a 2014 study of a five-day outward-bound programme in Singapore on 136 adolescent truants found improved attendance of both academic and non-academic activities three months after the conclusion of the programme. In 2008, researcher Emily Cook found boys, aged between twelve and sixteen, who took part in a residential wilderness programme showed more sociable behaviour four months later. The vast majority (92 per cent) who had noted a problem with social skills indicated that the programme had helped them with their relationships with others back home. The participants stated, 'I am being more mature with people and not as hyper. I can control myself much better', 'I don't argue as much. I have learnt to bring things to people without yelling' and 'I have been doing a ton better on my anger management'. This may be due to the support shown from peers in rising to the challenges of the programme, where they hiked the Appalachian Trail. In the words of one of the boys, 'you help each other out and the group comes back a whole lot more supportive of each other'.

And when it comes to academic learning, students do better with adventure, too. According to John Hattie's adventure-education report, 65 per cent of adventure-programme students exceeded those not participating at a 15 per cent improved rate of learning. Further studies have shown that participants learnt more, they learnt faster and, in particular, their problem-solving competencies were enhanced. According to the Education Endowment Foundation, collaborative outdoor adventure education, such as climbing, sailing and canoeing, consistently shows positive benefits on academic learning – on average it has been proven to add approximately four months' educational attainment to a child's progress over a single year. It's worth noting that this compares to five months' additional academic progress attained from one-to-one tuition.

Evidently, adventure matters because it helps us to think better, feel better and do better. It helps us to be well. Given that, as the 2015 World Happiness Report states, 'happiness and wellbeing are best regarded as skills that can be enhanced through training', adventure can be seen as a critical part of that training. Less, however, is known about *why* adventure benefits us. Finding out will enable us to use it much more effectively in our own lives and in society, and I believe a relatively new field of psychology may offer some answers.

A theory of wellbeing

Positive psychology (the study of optimal human functioning) is a relatively modern field. Until 1995, psychology had traditionally focused on getting people from mentally ill back to neutral. Positive psychology focuses on getting people from neutral to flourishing or as Chris Peterson, one of the founders of the field, described it, 'north of neutral'. This is critical to how I see the Adventure Revolution, because I'm not just arguing for the use of adventure as a therapy for those with mental illness, which has predominantly been the focus of research in the past. Adventure is in fact a necessity for *everyone*; we *all* need it in our lives to truly reach our potential and optimal wellbeing. Assessing the evidence using a positive-psychology lens is useful in further understanding the Adventure Effect and how it can help us all to flourish.

One of the founders of positive psychology, Martin Seligman, developed a theory of wellbeing, known as the PERMA model, which identifies five independent components:

- Positive emotion
- Engagement
- Relationships
- Meaning
- Accomplishment

Happiness, the traditional measure of life satisfaction, is merely a fleeting feeling. Instead, if we wish to achieve optimal wellbeing, we need to have the presence of all five components of PERMA in our lives.

Adventure supports every single one of these elements of wellbeing. Let's have a look at each of them in the context of adventure.

Positive emotion

Positive emotions are a prime indicator of flourishing and they can be cultivated or learned to improve wellbeing. The main positive emotions include: joy, interest, love, gratitude, serenity, hope, pride, amusement, inspiration and awe. Adventure facilitates the feeling of many of these. For example, adventure can instil us with much pride as we overcome obstacles and achieve goals. The striving of our resilient teammates and exotic surroundings can cause us to feel awestruck and inspired. Serenity can be reached as you savour the moments away from the modern world's noise and worries and simply focus on putting one foot in front of the other, while much joy and hope can come from planning and going on adventures and reminiscing afterwards as we reflect on what we've achieved.

Adventure induces all kinds of positive emotions, even when maybe it shouldn't. For example, in a study by Paula Reid and Hanna Kampman investigating why adventurers adventure, one interviewee, who had cycled 14,000 miles, talked about how stripping himself back from luxuries had made him the happiest he'd ever been, so much so that he remembered lying in a ditch, dirty, 'I've near enough used all the money for the house that I didn't get. I was in this ditch on my tod, and I was the most happiest I've ever been in my entire life.'

Engagement

Engagement is about being so absorbed by an activity that you lose track of time. In order to feel truly engaged, you must be sufficiently challenged by what you face but not so challenged that it becomes frustrating or impossible. The intensity of the experience means you are fully immersed in the present moment. So much so that nothing else matters – only what you are doing now and next, each footprint and handhold and sensation is felt deeply and can bring about almost a meditative quality of focus on the now. When you enter a new world via adventure and leave normal life behind for a while, you are choosing to face challenges of mind and body and a period of total immersion. This freedom from everyday concerns and engagement in the adventure alone is a calm place to be; it's no wonder it bolsters wellbeing.

Positive emotion can be reached by effortless shortcuts (watching TV, taking drugs, going shopping), but there are no shortcuts to full engagement or 'flow'. On the contrary, you need to maximise your talents and perseverance to play an instrument, take part in a sport, make progress with an interesting work project – and that is how you stretch your intelligence and skills, and identify your greatest strengths.

Relationships

Strong, supportive and rewarding social relationships are critical to our wellbeing. Adventure has been shown to deepen our connections with the people we're adventuring with, and if adventuring solo, to deepen our connection with ourselves. Feelings of camaraderie are generated by being together during moments of great challenge and vulnerability, like the boys walking the Appalachian Trail together in Emily Cook's study. People develop their social skills, such as teamwork, group cohesion, leadership and empathy, along with improved trust of and communication with each other, while embarking on adventures together.

And it's not only our relationships with the people we're adventuring with that are positively affected; it's our connections with those in our lives back home too. For example, in her survey of female adventurers, Hetty Key found that outdoor adventures helped women to strengthen friendships, experience increased empathy in their everyday lives, and it had a knock-on effect in terms of how family time was spent.

Meaning

A growing body of research has found that the feeling that one's life has meaning (purpose and significance), that you serve something that is bigger than yourself, is associated with a host of positive mental and physical health outcomes. For

example, a 2019 study of older adults found that meaningful-
ness in life was linked to less loneliness, stronger relationships
and even less obesity. Similarly, the 2012 report 'Purpose, Mood
and Pleasure in Predicting Satisfaction Judgements' linked a
strong sense of purpose with higher levels of self-esteem.

Adventure is purposeful to the core. When you go on an
adventure, whether your purpose is to climb something,
hike from A to B or secure scientific results, you have a clear
goal that gives your days, and your expedition, meaning. But
more than the purpose of the task of adventure, the whole
experience can positively impact how significant your life
feels. The act of finding out what is possible and what you
are capable of can generate meaning, so rising to a challenge
is an important activity in itself.

Accomplishment

Having goals in life can push us to achieve things that can
give us a sense of accomplishment. Simply striving for those
goals can give a sense of satisfaction, but when you do
succeed, a great sense of pride and fulfilment is reached.
Challenge and achievement are intrinsically linked.
Adventure offers the perfect opportunity to strive for a goal
– to summit a mountain, to navigate a river, to rise to a challenge. This serves as a perpetual loop of motivation, as each
time you rise to a challenge you feel a sense of achievement,
which spurs you on to reach further. Certainly, I've found
adventure has enabled me to discover what I'm capable of,
to find my own mental and physical limits and then push
through them to achieve more. According to peer reviews,
participants in Outward Bound activities always achieve
more than they believed they were capable of and, as a direct

consequence, have higher aspirations and expectations for the future, just as the teenagers in Emily Cook's study who had manifested low self-esteem noted an improvement in how they saw themselves and their futures as a result of the programme.

So, there is testimony, evidence and theory to support the Adventure Effect. It's almost as if adventure was created by professors of positive psychology to bring all the elements of wellbeing together into one easy-to-administer dose of flourishing. We just need to pay attention to the evidence, listen to our instincts and take the medicine. But let's not forget why it matters: it's the power of adventure to transform people and change their lives for the better.

In 2009, experienced charity manager Joe Taylor was asked to help set up a surf school for people with disabilities near Newquay in Cornwall. He was surprised and impressed at the impact the surfing had on the participants, and it gave him the idea to set up a pilot scheme offering surf therapy nearby at Watergate Bay in 2010. Ten years later, I spoke to Joe about how his initial idea had sparked such incredibly positive change for children across the United Kingdom through a system of social prescribing, which involves health professionals referring patients to support services within the community, in order to improve their health and wellbeing.

Sam was one of the first troubled teenagers to be referred by the NHS's child and adolescent mental health team to Joe's pilot scheme. Sam had suffered from anxiety and depression so severe it had left him with selective mutism, which meant that even though he could speak, he never did. Joe hadn't heard of selective mutism before, nor did his course aim to cure the condition. 'All we offered Sam was an opportunity to try surfing in the hope that he might feel a bit better,' Joe explained. 'Surfing creates the idea of a sustained positive emotion. Falling off your board and getting back on again builds resilience. And being out in the waves is a very mindful experience.'

For six weeks, Sam learnt to surf, working one-to-one with his surf mentor, catching waves and trying to pop up. Over time, Sam relaxed; he laughed when he fell off his board, and he gestured wildly when he caught his first wave standing up. Then, at some otherwise unremarkable moment which suited him, Sam began to chat to his surf mentor.

When Sam's parents approached Joe after watching the last surf session, they didn't realise how many more lives were about to be transformed as a result of their words. Speaking in a quiet, serious voice, Sam's father said, 'We wanted to come and say thank you. You've given us back our son.'

'It was one of the most special moments of my life when I realised that something as simple as a surfing lesson could perform miracles,' said Joe, remembering this life-changing conversation. Just as the appreciation from Alice's mum left me in no doubt about what I wanted to do with the rest of my life, the grateful words of Sam's parents provided Joe with the catalyst to turn his Cornwall-based pilot surf-therapy course in Watergate Bay into The Wave Project, an adventure-based initiative that has since gone on to help transform the lives of thousands of children across the United Kingdom.

At a time when we perhaps need adventure more than ever, there has never been more evidence for its efficacy. Yet, just as adventure can have a powerfully positive and transformative effect, the lack of adventure can have an equally detrimental effect. From experience, I have seen what can happen when we go on adventures, but in researching this book, I've also discovered what can happen when we don't.

Three

The Absence of Adventure

'If you think adventure is dangerous, try routine, it's lethal.'
Paulo Coelho

I was told this story in 2015 by Ffyona Campbell, the first woman to walk around the world, as we swapped anecdotes about our time spent working with tribes.

A squad of Australian special-forces soldiers challenged an Aborigine tribe to a race across the outback to prove who was best at survival. They could carry whatever they wished and take whichever route they preferred, but they must travel solely on foot. Not surprisingly, the two teams approached the race differently. The soldiers were well equipped but weighed down with water, food, and camping and navigational equipment. The Aborigines packed just four sticks each: their spear, woomera (the rod for throwing their spear) and a hand-drill (two lengths of wood used to make fire through friction).

The soldiers and Aborigines were neck and neck until three quarters of the way into the race when the Aborigines went missing. As the soldiers arrived first at the finish line, they were bickering, sunburnt, exhausted and stressed, but they'd won the race.

Days later, the Aborigines were found sitting happily in the shade. They were all well and having fun, enjoying honeycomb together. During the race, one of them had realised they were near a spot where some honey would be ready, so they'd gone there instead and abandoned the race. They explained that eating honey in the shade was a much better way to spend their time than competing in a race across the desert.

The story of the race stayed with me for years. It neatly summed up my own experience of hunter-gatherer tribes and how their outlook on how to live their lives differs from our own in the modern world. It felt like it summarised something fundamental about what we might have lost.

The Aborigine tribe were free to venture off course, free to be playful and go with the flow, free to choose whatever most nourished and pleased them in the moment. Not only did they prove themselves to be best at survival (given that true survivors need to survive every day, not merely on race day), their flexibility and ability to live adventurously meant, while they didn't win the race, they did win at life. The regiment of special-forces soldiers meanwhile were restricted by rigid rules. They couldn't veer off course. Their aim was to win, to achieve, to succeed at all costs. As such, their experience was the epitome of how, in our modern world, progress has come at a cost.

We have an innate need to belong, so we dutifully follow rules and conform. This tendency has enabled humanity to build civilisations. We're told that by behaving like this we can create efficiency and achieve success, but we've some-how lost the balance along the way. We've sacrificed our freedom and our ability to embrace uncertainty for the illu-sion of control and the chance of society-sanctioned success. We've abandoned our natural ability to live adventurously and to dance to the beat of our own drum.

At times, I have felt that routine has made my life feel repetitive. The beep of the alarm. The stress of the commute. The rules of the road and the office. Check my teeth and hair before heading in for an unremarkable workday. After, get some exercise (maybe). Watch TV. Check social media (again). Eat, sleep, start again. Each day bleeds into the next. Many of us in industrial societies have experienced these routines, beset by rules, at some point in our lives.

Predictability and boredom have replaced uncertainty, so much so that we have become unaccustomed to the unknown or unplanned, even fearful of it. Instead of seeing the boundless opportunities within each unique day, a lack of certainty causes feelings of anxiety. This can lead us to live less boldly, limiting ourselves by avoiding challenge, under-estimating what we are capable of and taking fewer risks.

In 2014, teachers at the Richmond Avenue Primary and Nursery School in Essex made the decision to intentionally bring more risk to their campus. The schoolyard was trans-formed with crates, bricks, planks of wood and even a work-bench complete with tools. One of the teachers was quoted as saying, 'we have fires, we use knives, saws, different tools' all used under adult supervision. 'They normally only cut themselves once.' Educators at the school decided they needed to actively create risk for the children because the risky situations that used to come up in play naturally have been engineered out over decades of overprotection. Rather than making their school playground as safe as possible, they made it just as safe as necessary, because they had identified that risk-taking was essential for their students' development.

Over the past few decades, we've inflated bubbles around our kids and made everything 'safer'; for example, by banning traditional schoolyard games like tag, skipping and leapfrog. Safety and regulation have replaced fun and stimulation for what's being referred to as 'the bubble-wrap generation'. It seems the lunch break is, according to a researcher from Keele University, 'in danger of becoming a sterile, joyless time as schools over-react to an increasingly litigious society'. Given what we now know (and will explore more in the following chapter) about risk-taking bolstering our resilience, wrapping ourselves and our children in cotton wool is doing more harm mentally than good.

We've put so much emphasis on health and safety over recent years to the detriment of risk, but I believe we need to find a balance between mental health and safety. Our increasing litigiousness and obsession with physical safety at all costs have helped to plant and grow seeds of fear, sometimes irrational ones. This fear has even made us crueller: our increasingly risk-averse society is less likely to show kindness and will often avoid helping someone in trouble for fear of being sued.

This attitude to risk no longer just shows up in our urban spaces; it's in our last wildernesses too. Across Europe and the USA, land managers such as the Forest Service and National Park Service are being deemed as 'responsible' for fatalities caused by natural tragedies (for example, falling trees, storm-flooded rivers, animal attacks) which have happened on their turf. The knock-on effect is for them to act to mitigate the risks to visitors' safety by putting up fences and signs all over the place, intruding on our landscapes and impeding our freedom, keeping people away from the cliffs and lakes, just in case. This modern mentality, where grown adults are spoon-fed, even in the wilderness, reached a crisis point when, in 2017, much to the dismay of many mountaineers, Jean-Marc Peillex, the mayor of the region, made it illegal to climb Mont Blanc without a specific set of equipment (including helmet, ski mask, harness, rope and ice axe). No such regulation has ever existed on any of the world's mountains before, because mountains are by their very nature uncontrollable.

Imposing man-made laws on mountain tops and confusing wild spaces with urban ones will likely generate less responsible behaviour and even more lawsuits for land managers unable to protect individuals in natural settings. Weirdly, the more 'equipped' we are with rules and regulations, the more stripped we are of our own responsibility for our safety. The less practice people have at taking risks, the worse they become at managing them; the less responsibility people are given for their own safety, the less they know *how* to stay safe.

We've examined how the drive for efficiency has made life more predictable and us less accustomed to dealing with uncertainty. The increasing focus on keeping safe has made us less confident to manage risk. But there is another factor that has kept us from living adventurously, and this is inextricably linked to our move indoors.

How did we get here?

'By respecting our inner hunter-gatherer, we can much improve our urban wellbeing.'

Gustav Milne, archaeologist

Probably the biggest change in lifestyle over the last ten thousand years is our move from wild, uncontrollable, uncertain nature in the great outdoors to spending most of our time in a safe, thermostatically controlled and comfortable indoor environment. In fact, the only time many of us see 'Adventure' is following the words 'Action &' as we scroll through Netflix from our sofas. The National Human Activity Pattern Survey published by the Lawrence Berkeley National Laboratory in 2001 found that American adults spend 87 per cent of their time indoors. We've gone from being an outdoor species to an indoor species. And this has now become official: *Homo sapiens* became an urban species in 2009, when statistics from the United Nations revealed that for the first time more people were living in urban than rural areas around the world.

With more brain power than our forebears, we *Homo sapiens* came up with one clever idea after another to survive. Perhaps most importantly, we began to adapt the environment to suit us, rather than the other way around. The inventions of fur-skin clothing, stone tools and mastery of fire led to the start of agriculture 10,000 years ago. Farming and husbandry meant settling down to tend our flocks and crops, which meant far less hunting, gathering and nomadic wandering. By the time of the Industrial Revolution, just 200 years ago, human lifestyles had changed to include heating, indoor plumbing, mass production of food and other conveniences of modern life. In the mere blink of an eye in evolutionary time, we went from living off the land in nomadic tribes to sitting in front of screens for work and for pleasure, ordering dinner delivery from the small electronic device we each keep in our pockets.

This colossal change in how we live explains the rise of predictability and comfort. But I believe it also gives us a clue as to why our lack of adventure has poorly affected our wellbeing and why adventurous outdoor challenges are such potent medicine: our bodies and minds were made for them.

Adventurous by design

'The things we have made to keep us comfortable are making us weak.'

Wim Hof

The human body and mind have been shaped by millions of years of evolution, during which time, the various species that preceded us lived as hunter-gatherers. That's millions of years of evolution spent honing minds and bodies to live off the land and to thrive in the challenging and ever-changing natural environment. *Homo sapiens*, the first modern humans, evolved from these hominid predecessors around 300,000 years ago. Since then, the human body has evolved to be a little smaller and now exhibits regional variation, but, essentially, our bodies are very similar to those first humans.

Take, for instance, your manager. You know the one. He wears a suit, talks about 'idea showers' and sips a skinny soy latte each morning. Even he, physiologically, has essentially

the same body and mind as the Palaeolithic caveman ances-
tor who battled mastodons with nothing more than cunning,
wits and a pointed stick. (And I know who I'd put money on
in a match against a mastodon.) Your manager, though, has
been raised in relative safety and comfort. He sleeps in a bed,
with pillows and blankets. He works in air-conditioned
rooms and drives his air-conditioned car to 'hunt down'
food at the supermarket. While our bodies and minds haven't
changed much over the last 300,000 years, our way of life has
altered dramatically.

As our environment has changed faster than our bodies
have, there is now a mismatch between what our bodies and
minds have evolved to be and do, and the environment we
have created. Our bodies and minds aren't adapted to live in
boxes, to sit in front of screens, our daily worries revolving
around whether we'll get a parking space close enough or an
exam grade good enough. Nor were our bodies and minds
built to live such sedentary indoor lifestyles. Rather, we were
born to adventure outdoors, to face uncertainty, to hunt and
to gather and to move.

There's a discrepancy between our present lifestyle and
the one our genes were selected for, and the poor fit is
making us unwell. This is evolutionary mismatch.

A 1997 study into Paleolithic nutrition tells us that the
daily average energy expenditure of our ancestors was
around 3,000 to 5,000 calories, as they moved at least ten
miles per day. Furthermore, not only did our invariably
leaner ancestors move more, they did so outdoors in the
fresh air, rather than lined up in gyms. And they toiled
outside too, rather than hunched over desks. They enjoyed
better quality sleep due to their active lifestyles and

maintained their vitamin D levels, which enhanced their ability to absorb important nutrients.

The convenience of working, shopping and being entertained from the comfort of our chairs means we are moving considerably less. We have used our oversized brains to shape the world around us and to develop tools and technology to successfully rid ourselves of the deprivations faced by our ancestors, but our bodies aren't stronger. On the contrary, we are larger, slower and less fit. Excess has replaced deficiency. Large swathes of the population merely move from the driver's seat to the office chair to the sofa and into bed (and repeat). This has led to soaring rates of obesity, type 2 diabetes and heart disease in Western countries: one in every four American deaths is caused by heart disease, two out of every three adults in the UK is either overweight or obese, and one Australian citizen develops diabetes every five minutes.

Researchers from the Centre for Primary Health Care Research at Lund University in Sweden found that the 'mismatch between our ancient physiology and the western diet and lifestyle underlies many so-called diseases of civilisation, including coronary heart disease, obesity, hypertension, type 2 diabetes, epithelial cell cancers, autoimmune disease, and osteoporosis, which are rare or virtually absent in hunter-gatherers and other non-westernized populations'.

The link between inactivity, poor nutrition and ill health is well evidenced, but there is increasing evidence that our bodies are also suffering because they are no longer subjected to the extremes and hardships of an adventurous outdoor lifestyle. Eternal homeostasis is not what we were built for. We are wired to live in challenging and changing environments, to regularly experience heat, tiredness, hunger, thirst and cold. Recent studies have shown that reintroducing these stressors can help improve our health by triggering biological responses in our body that have lain dormant.

For example, a 2020 study from the University of Cambridge showed that cold-water swimming may protect the brain from degenerative diseases. The researchers found a 'cold-shock' protein in the blood of regular winter swimmers, which has been shown to slow the onset of dementia and even repair some of the damage it causes. The research centres on the hibernation ability that all mammals retain, which is prompted by exposure to cold. Emerging evidence also suggests beneficial effects from taking saunas. A group of researchers from the University of Eastern Finland have found, over a series of studies from 2015 to 2017, that people who regularly spend time in hot, dry saunas had lower rates of hypertension and dementia and lived longer compared to infrequent users, and that taking saunas can have a direct effect on blood pressure, heart rate and vascular health. There is also evidence to suggest we benefit from occasionally experiencing hunger. In 2014, researchers from the Longevity Institute at the University of Southern California found that intermittent or periodic fasting amongst adult humans helps reduce obesity, hypertension, asthma and rheumatoid arthritis.

The idea of reintroducing the stressors our forebears experienced into our comfortable modern lives to improve physical health has been put into practice by extreme athlete Wim Hof, known as 'The Iceman'. He has added common environmental adversities to his daily life, such as excess cold (through regular ice-cold plunges), heat (by taking daily saunas) and hunger (though periodic fasting), and he has restored his physical evolutionary vigour so much so that he has run a half marathon above the Arctic Circle barefoot only wearing shorts, been submerged in ice cubes for more than 112 minutes and run a full marathon in the Namib Desert without drinking.

As our bodies were designed to be active and our feet were designed to run barefoot, so too our brains were designed to cope with adversity and to constantly adapt to challenges in an unpredictable world. Rising to these challenges gave us the chance to build our muscle and bone strength but also to create more neurons, synapses and brain tissue, while simultaneously gaining new and sustaining existing skills.

In his book *Sapiens: A Brief History of Humankind*, Yuval Noah Harari notes that 'the human collective knows far more today than did the ancient bands. But at the individual level, ancient foragers were the most knowledgeable and skilful people in history'. Our Palaeolithic ancestors needed to have in-depth knowledge of the natural world: how to find, identify and prepare edible plants, forecast weather or natural disasters such as avalanches, be in tune with the habits of their predators and prey. They also needed to master multiple skills through years of apprenticeship in order to survive, from crossing rivers to evading bears and catching fish. I've been struck by how the Hadza hunter-gatherers from Tanzania could sense animals in the forest way before I'd see them, not just knowing something was there but knowing what kind of animal, its size and what it was doing or its direction of travel. It felt like they had a sixth sense. I also saw it in the way a San bushman brought me to water. Walking through miles of desert scrub, each direction looking identical, he stopped and started digging.

There were no distinguishing plants, rocks, anything to mark this spot; it was indistinguishable from the miles of scrub surrounding it. But after more than thirty minutes of digging, the sand began to come out of the ground wet instead of dry, and after another thirty minutes, we had water to drink. Hunter-gatherers are challenged daily, making them masters of their environment, and with this must come huge feelings of accomplishment.

In order to build civilisations, humans, individually, have needed to specialise, to become experts in their niche, because this improves the overall efficiency of our societies. The outcome is that as individuals we have fewer skills, because we've trained for a reduced range of attributes. You could say we are therefore challenged in less varied and acute ways, and we are also less self-reliant than ever before. We need only to know how to be a physics teacher, an insurance salesman or an office manager to survive. We rely blindly on other experts for most of our necessities. I know very few people who can build their own house, grow their own food and make their own clothes.

The challenge of adventure has taught me to embrace learning, far more than the pressure of 'passing exams', which mostly promoted anxiety. I've not taken up a new adventure without learning huge amounts about the world. When I rowed around Britain, I learnt how to navigate at sea, recognise patterns of weather and water movement, tie knots, deploy anchors, execute and recognise maritime protocols, fix valves, maintain water purifiers – the list goes on. When I sailed around and across the Atlantic, I carried out weeks of training before I could join the rest of the crew. Living adventurously is the ultimate teacher.

There is something uniquely rewarding in building self-reliance, especially in the outdoors. Modern humans by comparison to our hunter-gatherer ancestors are largely helpless in the wilderness, especially without our navigational equipment, specialist clothing and other modern accoutrements. I've felt great pride in mastering how to live and work in different environments: how to hang your hammock in a jungle or how to site the camp by looking out for potential deadfall (trees that might collapse), flooding signs or animal nests. Learning, sometimes the hard way, how to navigate in near-featureless deserts or find water. The pride is different to that of getting a good grade or a promotion; it's somehow more tangible. Rather than achieving something that simply compares me to others, it's just me and the elements. It's elemental. And I've seen it in others too: every time I teach someone how to light a campfire for the first time, whether they are a child or a CEO, I recognise their look of sheer delight.

Adventurous activity is an opportunity to build our self-reliance in the most primal ways and stretch our brains to learn things completely outside of our usual everyday lives and careers. This can bring feelings of pride and accomplishment. Adding adventure can also help us to relieve the constant stress and worry of twenty-first-century living.

While life has in many ways become less varied and less exciting, compared to that lived by our Palaeolithic ancestors, it has also become, in some regards at least, *more* rather than less stressful. We live a safer and more comfortable existence, and we do not have to worry about predators, hunger or extreme weather on a regular basis, which is of course real progress, but I believe this comes at a cost in terms of our levels of chronic stress.

In 2018, stress accounted for nearly half of all sick days in the UK and was estimated to cost American businesses up to $300 billion a year. A Mental Health Foundation poll in 2018 alarmingly revealed that as many as 74 per cent of people in England had felt so stressed over the previous year that they had been overwhelmed or unable to cope. Hence why the World Health Organization has declared stress the modern health epidemic of the twenty-first century.

Our stress response – fight or flight – evolved at a time where the danger of physical assault by dangerous predators was a daily possibility. But the pace of progress in eradicating that threat has not been matched by our own evolution, so our stress response still reacts as if there could be a woolly mammoth lurking around the corner.

Genuine threats to our safety experienced when we were all hunter-gatherers triggered a primal fight or flight response in our bodies, releasing stress hormones that sped through our bloodstreams and primed us to be super alert, ready to evade danger and improve our chances of survival. Our reaction times increased and our concentration became more focused, and then, when the threat had passed, our inbuilt stress responses switched off and our bodies and minds returned to normal, satisfied and sometimes euphoric. On the whole, we experienced intense but relatively brief bursts of acute stress like this followed by longer periods of relief, relaxation and satisfaction.

This fight or flight response still exists in our bodies, but there is a mismatch between it and our modern stressors. For many of us, the lack of predators and flash floods leave us with nothing to worry about, so we worry about everything. Our minds search for danger where there is none or focus on future worries. In civilised modern society, we face challenges that are different to our forebears; these include trying to achieve future-based goals, like moving house, passing exams or obtaining the next promotion. Our never-ending to-do lists and nonstop notifications keep us perpetually on edge. On top of this, social feeds perpetuate the rising pressure from media and society to succeed, achieve and look good. The result is constant worry, and the stress hormones build up and stay at chronic levels in our body. There's no peak, but there's also no relief.

If you consider the levels of stress hormones in the human body, the varied peaks and troughs that dance through a hunter-gatherer lifestyle compares starkly with the constant levels of worry that define many of our modern days. If hunter-gatherer life is exemplified by more ups and downs, modern life by comparison could be seen to be flatlining.

This mismatch is causing us harm as the fight-or-flight response that once protected our ancestors from sporadic events runs on overdrive in our modern lives. Our brains weren't designed to deal with constant stress; they were designed to cope with brief bursts of acute stress. Research now shows that long-term activation of the stress system, in particular constant levels of cortisol, can have a hazardous, even lethal, effect on the body, increasing risk of obesity, heart disease, depression and a variety of other illnesses.

It seems we've created modern lifestyles that counter what our minds were designed to do. A hunter-gatherer lifestyle that is defined by exploration, opportunistic problem-solving and play has been replaced by a modern approach characterised by planning, duty and discipline. Leading molecular biologist John Medina agrees this mismatch goes to a molecular level:

> The brain appears to be designed to solve problems related to surviving in an unstable outdoor environment, and to do so in nearly constant motion ... If you wanted to create an education environment that was directly opposed to what the brain was good at doing, you probably would design something like a classroom. If you wanted to create a business environment that was directly opposed to what the brain was good at doing, you probably would design something like a cubicle. And if you wanted to change things, you might have to tear down both and start over.

No wonder people might feel an urge to escape the cubicles, routines and rules, maybe even find a wilder way to live.

The story of Hope Bourne captivated me when I first heard it in 2015, and I suspect it was unconsciously instrumental in drawing me to Exmoor, one of the last places in England that still feels wild, and our home since 2017. In 1970, at the age of fifty-two, Hope Bourne began her greatest adventure. Seeking a self-sufficient life surrounded by nature, she moved into a tiny, old, leaky caravan by the burnt-out ruins of Ferny Ball Farm in the heart of Exmoor. She lived there alone for twenty-four years. She shot rabbit, hare, pigeon and the occasional deer. She grew her own vegetables, fished, drank from the streams and kept bantams in the ruined buildings. She helped out on the neighbouring farms at busy times in exchange for shooting and fishing rights. Her days were filled with writing, painting and gardening, and she went for a twenty-mile walk with her sketchpad every day.

But she had had a rather less wild start in life. Hope was born in Oxford in 1918 but grew up in Hartland in North Devon, where her mother was headmistress at the village school. Hope left school at the age of fourteen, and as the only child of a widowed mother, she was expected to stay at home. Her mother died when Hope was in her thirties, leaving her with no income, home or qualifications, so she decided to become as self-sufficient as possible. Hope moved to Exmoor and lived in a succession of remote and primitive cottages, living off the land until she moved to her Ferny Ball ruins in 1970.

Hope turned her back on modern life for something simpler and more adventurous. 'I can't stand towns,' she said. 'I see all the little houses like little boxes and everything planned out, laid out, safe and ordered – well, there's no adventure in it, no excitement, no anything.' She disapproved of bureaucracy and over-industrialisation and wanted her beloved Exmoor National Park to be left alone. If she'd had her way, she'd have removed the car parks, way-marked footpaths and information signs. She described her life as 'a good life but it's a tough life. You've got to be 100 per cent physically fit to live as I do. You've got to be tough, body and soul. Whatever happens at Ferny Ball, I've got to cope with it alone.' Hope was a champion for Exmoor but also for defending our untamed wild places, places where you can live adventurously. 'For money, you sell the hours and the days of your life, which are the only true wealth you have,' she wrote. 'You sell the sunshine, the dawn and the dusk, the moon and the stars, the wind and the rain, the green fields and the flowers, the rivers and the sweet fresh air. You sell health and joy and freedom.'

Hope was part of our inspiration to move to Exmoor National Park, a place of dark skies and rugged moors, where we could have adventures and raise our son in relative wilderness. We weren't just seeking somewhere 'greener' to live; we were seeking somewhere 'wilder'. We now live just a few miles from where Hope lived at Ferny Ball.

Although I wouldn't choose to live quite as Hope did, it's impossible not be to inspired by the way she lived on her own terms. Stories of people returning to the wild captivate me, and countless others, not just because they are intriguing, but I think because they speak to an inner hunter-gatherer desire many of us have to be more self-sufficient, adventurous and free. Who's to say that the 'extreme' way Hope lived is any better or worse than the 'extreme' way many of us live, in rule-bound comfort? Maybe the answer is finding our own balance between the two, and that's why many of us who have experienced the convenience and routine of modern life welcome the disruption of a little added adventure.

Research increasingly shows the negative effect evolutionary mismatch is having on our physical and mental health. To resolve the conflict between the modern environment and our ancient genome, the growing consensus amongst researchers is that we should adopt elements of a lifestyle that mimics the beneficial characteristics of the Palaeolithic era.

Our ancestors walked the earth for millennia, bound only by the laws of nature. Their lives essentially *were* adventure, filled with uncertainty and danger, but also with variety, freedom and challenge. I'm not suggesting we return to that lifestyle, or even close to it, like Hope did – after all, our ancestors did everything they could to escape the stressors they were experiencing. They had no choice, but we do.

Intentionally introducing adventurous activity could offer relief from the stress of modern life as well as providing ways for us to learn and grow as individuals. Adventure is a particularly good fit to our current societal problems. It can give us a route out of chronic stress, replacing it with times of acute stress and relief, which makes us feel alive. And it can give us a chance to use our brains as they were designed to be used, allowing us to build skills, confidence and deep feelings of accomplishment.

As someone who has a tendency to over-worry myself, I've used adventure as a respite from the constant pressures of the modern world. Before you leave on the adventure, you have a million and one things to do, but as soon as you set foot on the plane, sit on the seat of your bike or turn away from your car with a full backpack, life immediately becomes so much simpler. Any nagging feelings dissipate and are replaced by something more exciting: the challenge, the unknown, demanding you to be alert, engaged, committed. Ironically, the times when I have found most peace have been cutting through a dense jungle or facing the elements out at sea, times that others assume I must have been most stressed. Instead, during those moments I'm enveloped in a feeling of calm and purpose. It is my escape from chronic stress, and it's my path to personal growth through the Adventure Effect. And then of course there's the payoff too: you notice and take time to celebrate the big and small victories when the background buzz is no longer there to distract you. You can experience moments of true achievement. Jen, a member of Explorers Connect, explained to me how she took her friend Simon, who was a cocaine addict and in a 'very dark place', hiking in the Peak District. He was very apprehensive and thought he wouldn't be able to keep up, but she encouraged him to persevere. They walked eight miles to the top of Dove Stones, and when he reached the viewpoint, he said that he felt like he was 'naturally high' and that it was far better than the high from cocaine. Since then, he's replaced some of his cocaine habit with a hiking habit – maybe one day he'll replace it altogether.

In a drive to be more efficient, we've set up a system of rules that have removed uncertainty and promote living predictability. Additionally, we've produced invention after invention to make our lives easier and more convenient, to help us to do things, get places and achieve goals faster. Sadly, an absence of adventure has become our new normal in a risk-averse, comfortable society beset by regulations. But it's time we shake off the restrictions and, while still taking care of our safety, seek out challenge, learn to embrace uncertainty and allow ourselves to thrive.

Four

To Heal

'I feel beneath the white. There is a redskin suffering. From centuries of taming.'

'Kings of the Wild Frontier', Adam Ant

'I'd be dead if I didn't have an expeditionary mindset.'

This was the first thing Phil Coates said when he called me out of the blue in 2019. I'd met Phil at the RGS many years earlier when we'd worked together on some adventure projects. He'd travelled around the world multiple times and had worked in some of the most extreme places on the planet, specialising in high altitude and high Arctic.

Now, after sustaining a traumatic brain injury, compression on his cerebellum, he was in Royal Buckinghamshire Hospital, having spent the last ten months in a wheelchair learning how to talk again. You might have thought, given all his years of rugged adventuring in the most extreme environments in the world, that he'd sustained this injury on an endurance expedition of some kind. But he hadn't.

Phil had slipped and fallen in the shower in a hotel in leafy Surrey.

Despite his slurred speech, Phil's sharp wit, charm and intellect still shone through. Following the worst year of his life, Phil explained what he'd been through: 'It's like living every day of my life in the death zone on Everest.' He'd spent the past five months relearning how to use a knife just so he could add vegetables to his noodle-based meals.

In the early weeks after his accident, he'd heard the nursing auxiliary say they hadn't been sure whether to get the stretcher gurney or the body bag when they'd picked him up, such was the extent of his injury. Understandably, Phil had felt desperate about what lay ahead and hadn't been sure whether he'd be able to cope: 'I didn't know how dark my future might be. So, as I watched the matron open the window latches in my bedroom, I memorised how I could repeat the action, get out of my wheelchair prison and leave the building five floors up.' Phil was certain that had he not built his resilience during his Arctic expeditions, he would've 'just jumped out of the window'. His experience up the north side of Everest and beyond stopped him jumping out of that window because he knew he was capable of enduring the worst and coming out the other side.

'Without the skills I'd learnt to survive above 8,000 metres, I wouldn't have kept going ... Just having a drink of water at high altitude or in the Arctic takes diligence and determination. Above 8,000 metres, you are in the death zone, and you are slowly dying, so everything is laboured. Even heating snow to make water is a colossal lesson in effort. Without that background I'd be buggered, and I'm sure I'd have given up.' Phil still has a long way to go, but little by little he is learning how to live again. He was able to use his past experiences of adventure to bolster his current resilience.

Psychological resilience is our human capacity to cope with a crisis or hardship, to respond effectively to challenges and to bounce back accordingly. The word comes from the Latin *resilire*, to jump back, to return to pre-crisis status quickly. Resilience exists in people who develop psychological and behavioural capabilities that protect them from potential long-term negative effects of life's stressors. Adventure provides ample opportunity to practise flexing our resilience muscles and, in doing so, to make them stronger.

This sentiment is echoed by respondents to the Women in Adventure survey, one of whom explained how adventure had boosted her wellbeing: 'Overcoming physical challenges outdoors has shown me I have more resilience than I ever knew. I finally feel that I have a valid place in the world and am connected to the planet that I live on. The outdoors gives me a place where I feel like I belong.' And there's a wide range of studies to back this up.

In their report 'Adventure Education and Resilience: The Double-edged Sword' in the *Journal of Adventure Education and Outdoor Learning*, J. T. Neil and K. L. Dias measured gains in resilience in a group of forty-one young adults participating in a twenty-two-day outward-bound programme in Australia. Typical activities included expedition and food planning, navigation, caving, rafting, climbing and abseiling. The researchers noted 'a very large effect' on the levels of resilience on every single one of the participants. In 2020, researchers from Leeds Beckett University carried out a survey of 2,500 new students as they took the important step of starting higher education. The report not only found an improved resilience in the students that undertook a five-day adventure residential, they found their resilience was still significantly improved three months later. The Leeds Beckett researchers state that their findings support the idea that 'outdoor adventure supports developing the adaptive skills which enable inductees to make successful lasting transitions'.

Although no studies have been carried out that can refute or support the long-lasting benefits of adventure entirely, there have been some encouraging reports that point in this direction. For example, in 2016 the National Child Development Study, a multidisciplinary study which follows the lives of 17,415 people born in the United Kingdom in March 1958, found that about a quarter of the study participants had been in the Scouts or Guides, and this group was around 15 per cent less likely to go on to suffer from anxiety or mood disorders at age fifty. The lead researcher Professor Chris Dibben commented that 'it is quite startling that this benefit is found in people so many years after'. He suggests that attending Scouts or Guides may help build resilience against everyday stresses and make children more determined and capable in achieving their goals, even many years later.

More evidence comes from Outward Bound, a charity founded by Kurt Hahn in 1941. Hahn had noticed that young soldiers weren't as able to deal with adversity as older, more experienced ones. The reason, it turned out, was that the younger soldiers hadn't experienced adversity and so didn't know how to deal with it. The charity has, over the past eighty years, used a 'development-by-challenge philosophy' to help children face difficulties they didn't think they could and draw on untapped strengths to defy limitations and overcome obstacles. In its 2019 Mental Health and Resilience Report, the organisation reported that these children become at least three times more resilient, more determined and more confident than children in a non-participating control group. And this helps explain how adventure builds resilience. Hahn described the adventure-education process as 'like a double-edged sword which cuts a person and then heals stronger than before'.

I asked Professor Alan Ewert, one of the leading experts in the adventure psychology field, to speak about resilience at my conference Adventure Mind in 2020. He explained how 'in a sense and particularly with reference for contemporary society, using adventure to develop resilience is analogous to using a vaccine; that is, it can strengthen or harden the individual for future adversity and challenge. This fact reminds us that the trail to developing resilience lies in successfully engaging challenge, not in avoiding it.'

The very nature of adventure involves the necessity to rise to challenges, overcome obstacles and persist in the face of adversity to achieve goals. Through figuring out ways to overcome the hurdles in their paths, adventurers become more resilient. They know they'll do whatever is required of them even in the toughest situations, because they've done so before – they've proven to themselves their bounce-back ability. And because adventure rewards resilience with achievement – that incredibly rewarding sense of accomplishment and relief when you reach the summit after a fifteen-hour trek – it's something adventurers never forget. If you've endured pain, the sense of achievement tastes even sweeter. And that's a useful resource to take back to your regular life. Because when you're going through something difficult, you can remind yourself that you've been through worse and keep going.

Phil was able to use his past experiences of adventure to bolster his current resilience. Meanwhile, others suffering from mental illness, trauma or behavioural problems may find that going on adventures helps them to find a road to recovery. This is the case with Danny, 'a short Scottish man built like a brick outhouse'. That's how my friend Al, an expedition logistician and medical expert, described him while I was on a remote first-aid course in 2008.

Danny was just how Al had portrayed him; his no-nonsense style of chat and short cropped hair testified to his military background. He also looked as tough as nails, a bit intimidating. But after just a couple of minutes talking with Danny, it was plain to see this gruff tough Scot had a proverbial heart of gold. He was also easy to spot, because he was holding what looked like bits of flesh with gaping wounds and protruding bones. These pros-thetics were used to add some true-to-life shock value to the first-aid scenarios on the course, and they did their job effectively. The scene should have been menacing, but what I remember most was this bull terrier of a man giving me a warm broad smile when I asked him about his work with drug addicts.

I had grown increasingly interested in the ways adventure was being used as therapy. I had read scientific papers on the subject but was more interested to hear stories that resonated and made sense to me. Outdoor adventure as an intervention wasn't mainstream at that time, but it was being used effectively with children, young offenders and with addicts. So, I was excited to hear that Danny was taking young addicts out into the wilderness on extreme micro-expeditions and 'curing' them.

While Danny smeared fake blood onto his colleague's leg, we talked about the kids he'd helped. Over a period of three summers, Danny had taken groups of young drug addicts from London to the wilds of Scotland. This had been no holiday, though. Instead, these struggling youths had undergone something more like military survival training, under Danny's guidance. On the first day in the wilderness, Danny had taught them how to build a shelter and start a fire, how to catch rabbits, forage plants and purify water. After a couple of shake-down days, the youths had been responsible for themselves. If they'd failed to set up traps or forage, they did not eat. And if they hadn't built their shelter properly, they had an uncomfortable, damp night. Danny had been there with them every step of the way as a mentor and a safety net, but he hadn't done any of these tasks for them. Ultimately, it was the difficulty of the challenge that had made it so effective.

Every single one of the young people Danny had sent back to London had stayed off drugs, a powerful example of the Adventure Effect. He had a 100 per cent track record of rehabilitation, compared to the success rate of therapy and other non-adventure-based interventions being between 20 and 60 per cent (for private residential rehabilitation) according to the NHS's National Treatment Agency for Substance Misuse in 2012. It was such a simple plan and surely one of the cheapest of interventions; besides some safety planning in advance, all he'd done was take them into the wilderness for an adventure and taught them the skills to survive.

In this way, adventure can be viewed as a remarkable tool for recovery. Danny reasoned his method works so well because he gives people personal responsibility. They learn to rely on themselves and their own skills, efforts and problem-solving abilities. Consequently, they learn they are more capable and resilient than they'd thought. This boosts their confidence levels but also makes them more willing to take responsibility for their own lives, decisions and outcomes, and more motivated to make good choices in the future. He described this as an accelerated 'growing up'.

Indeed, Danny's findings are backed up by science, as the learnt behaviour of addiction can be reset when an addict develops self-awareness and self-motivation and is able to unlearn bad habits and replace them with good ones. Furthermore, drug addiction often occurs as a means of coping with uncomfortable feelings or stress. When an addict discovers they can not only cope with these away from drug use but have proven their inner strength and resilience to themselves, they can more readily see that they no longer need to take drugs as a crutch or coping mechanism. While therapy is useful in equipping addicts with the mental tools to cope better, adventure shows them practically, out in the wilderness, that they are strong enough to take responsibility for their actions and overcome any challenges they face. Adventure-therapy challenges and team-building activities teach addicts that their choices impact others while bolstering their self-belief, giving them the coping skills they need to enable recovery and the confidence to stay sober and clean day by day.

Although adventure therapy is not yet well established in the UK or most of Europe, it's now being used extensively in several other countries, in particular the USA and Australia. The American Hospital Association recognises adventure therapy as a viable form of treatment, and the evidence to support its effectiveness is growing. As well as being used successfully in helping addicts to abstain from drug use, it is also shown to be an effective intervention for helping children recover from mental and physical illness, like the surfing therapy that helped Sam. A study published in the *Journal of Child and Family Studies* also showed that 95 per cent of troubled adolescents who participated in wilderness adventure therapy found the experience beneficial, with parents reporting huge behavioural and mindset improvements six weeks later. And the 2020 report 'Adventure Therapy for Child, Adolescent, and Young Adult Cancer Patients: A Systematic Review' found positive effects of adventure therapy on the physical activity, fatigue, psychological distress and quality of life of the youngsters.

Adventure therapy is also popular in helping service men and women to recover from post-traumatic stress disorder (PTSD). After a four-day adventure-training expedition in 2011, service men and women with PTSD reported reduced symptoms and greater coping ability, self-efficacy and confidence, while a 2013 study of veterans' experience on a nine-day climbing expedition saw participants report improvements in active coping, social support, determination and resilience. But, more than that, resilience can often lead us to bounce forward as well as bounce back – to become better and stronger than we were *before* the adversity. In fact, studies have shown that post-traumatic growth (PTG) leads to people becoming more appreciative, more creative and more purposeful following a traumatic experience. In essence, they become better able to cope and thrive not *despite* adversity but *because* they've gone through it.

There is also evidence that it can be effective for those who've suffered sexual abuse. In the book *Wilderness Therapy for Women: The Power of Adventure*, a thirty-year-old survivor of incest talks about how after her first wilderness experience 'I learnt to like my body again, it's not just for abuse, it's for other things, good things . . . I'm learning that it could be strong and that I can go hiking with it and do things that I love doing.'

Interestingly, an analysis of 197 reports in 2013 by D. Bowen and J. T. Neil showed that adventure-therapy studies have reported larger effects over time since the 1960s. I believe this is a sign of the times: adventure therapy is more effective now than in the past because we are more comfortable, less resilient and further divorced from adventure than at any other time in our history. The evidence is not yet conclusive, but the effectiveness of adventure therapy can't be ignored.

Adventure therapy may be defined as the prescriptive use of adventure experiences provided by mental-health professionals. However, we could consider it in an even wider context: I have found so many people, myself included, who 'self prescribe' adventure to help ourselves.

After enduring a decade of mental illness, low self-worth and an eating disorder, Beth Thomas discovered climbing as a route to recovery. In 2020, during the coronavirus pandemic, we talked about how she had happened upon her 'cure': 'Before climbing, I didn't feel connected to the world. I was trying to make sense of the point of life as there was so much angst and suffering related to being alive.' Beth had battled with bulimia for ten years from the age of thirteen. The illness reached a critical point at university, and she began to drink heavily: 'I felt unwelcome in the world, dirty and ashamed. This was definitely something that was not controllable for me until I realised that I would probably die if it continued.'

Her life took a turn for the better in her early twenties when she was given a 'learn to climb' course at an indoor wall and taught the basics: how to tie a figure of eight knot, how to belay, and how to stay safe. 'Climbing helps me focus,' she said. 'It encourages mindful thoughts and movements, and takes me away from the sometimes unhelpful mental chatter, which can be exhausting. Climbing movements are precise, all-consuming. I found I was calmer after a climbing session.' The course was short, but it gave Beth enough skills for her to begin top roping with a friend, and she then plucked up the courage to post an advert to find a climbing partner: 'We learnt to lead together, and I found, for the first time in years, that I felt confident and respectful of my body, especially when I was able to finish climbs I had previously only gawked at in bemusement.' A newly confident Beth booked herself onto a women-only five-day climbing holiday in Spain, which provided the catalyst for a more regular climbing routine. 'The more I climbed, the better I was feeling, mentally and physically,' Beth said. 'Climbing was something that challenged me, but in a way I didn't feel was unattainable or that I didn't belong. I felt a sense of deep personal satisfaction and achievement. I felt like suddenly there was a place for me and a purpose in moving my body that was nothing to do with weight loss. Climbing movement allowed me to appreciate the functionality of my body. You move in a four-dimensional way, up, down, forwards, backwards, twisting, etc. It is the natural type of movement we have evolved to survive. There's a real sense of dancing on the wall when you begin to listen to the body's natural way, dropping the knee, turning sideways to the wall, springing off your toes – you basically come home to your body.'

Beth continues to climb regularly. Having been in recovery for ten years, although dips in mood still occur, her mental health has remained stable and more manageable: 'Climbing put me back on track in life.' By using adventure as a response tool to regain mental focus and prove her ability to rise to challenges and achieve goals, Beth is staying on track and growing stronger.

Adventure teaches you that you can recover and heal. This was also the case for Amanda Challans, an inspirational woman I'd met through the social events I run for the Explorers Connect community. I've always had a particular interest in giving a platform to those who have turned their lives around through adventure, and since 2009 I've organised these gatherings where those interested in adventure are welcomed to meet, to inspire and assist each other towards more adventurous living. At a bar in Bristol in 2016, Amanda shared her amazing story with the like-minded crowd.

Growing up with her family in Devon, Amanda's childhood was filled with mini introductions to adventure: from weekend walks on Dartmoor and bundling the family into a tiny sailing boat to taking off in a caravan over the summer holidays to travel around Europe. The youngest in her class and dyslexic, Amanda struggled at school and, despite her best efforts, would constantly be called up on it. Then, one day, everything changed: 'This thing called "adventure training" came along – an extracurricular activity I could choose to sign up to alongside schoolwork. For the first time in my life, I felt I was naturally good at something.'

After leading the school's A-team on Ten Tors – a self-sufficient thirty-five-mile, two-day hike across Dartmoor – Amanda (then fifteen years old) and her team were greeted by national press, having succeeded in being the fastest all-girl team to finish. 'You could tell from our faces how much we'd bonded as a team and how unforgettable that weekend would remain to us all,' said Amanda, who promptly joined the Royal Navy Volunteer Cadet Corps. She signed up to every adventurous experience she could, from a month-long expedition in the Arctic to climbing mountains and sailing across the Arctic Ocean. Before long, Amanda was teaching courses to junior recruits to pass her own skills on.

Six years later, Amanda found herself in a very different setting. After a promising career in government and national security, Amanda's life began to fall apart. Hoping to qualify for the World Championships of Adventure Racing, Amanda collapsed during a qualifying round and spent the next four months in and out of doctors' surgeries and hospitals, undergoing forty different tests for cancer. Unable to work, she sold her car and her kayak to pay the rent, and finally, as a last resort, moved out of her London flat. Nine months later, doctors realised she'd had glandular fever, but since it hadn't been treated properly within the first few months, it had escalated to ME, otherwise known as chronic fatigue syndrome. Amanda was now bedbound or, on a good day, in a wheelchair, suffering from constant muscle pain and exhaustion, with the doctors offering no real medical understanding or cure and limited hope of recovery.

However, Amanda refused to accept this limiting prognosis. She knew a couple of people who had recovered from ME, a beacon of hope that she wouldn't let go of. Her background in adventure had prepared her with the resilience and determination to try to find a cure. And the promise of adventure itself was her inspiration: 'If there was a way out, a way back to a life of adventuring, I was determined to find it.' Whenever she had the energy, she trawled the internet to search for cures, but most of what she tried only made things worse: 'I'd try, fail, recover and try again.' One year after her diagnosis, she set a goal to be able to walk again. But six months later, she was just happy to be alive. 'My expectations were lowering all the time, until I had none,' Amanda said. 'No demands, only hope.'

Having significantly lowered her expectations, Amanda decided to set herself mini challenges and spent fifteen minutes each day writing a recipe book: 'Even though it was small, this gave me a sense of progress. Within a few months, I'd finished, and I still treasure and use it nine years on.' Setting mini challenges for herself in this way was something Amanda had learnt from her adventure training. It's a lesson I've learnt myself. In order to take on seemingly impossible challenges, you have to break them down into manageable steps. For example, rather than looking to the summit of Everest, you look to the first camp, reach it, then look to the next camp, and so on. This was the approach Amanda took to rebuilding her life, and after two years of refusing to give up hope and trying a plethora of different approaches, she'd started to recover.

Amanda's doctors reminded her that lots of people who've been through recovery can get ill again even years later, so Amanda lived in constant fear of her chronic fatigue returning. However, this emotional response was at odds with how she felt: 'I felt stronger than before and had become so in tune with my body. With this added awareness and all the information I'd studied on energy, I felt like I had even more potential than before.' That said, Amanda knew this was all theoretical, so she needed to prove it to herself. She sought out a new sport that wasn't associated with the time of her illness. Her sister suggested rowing, and before long, Amanda was out training five times a week and entering races. She wanted to push herself further than she'd ever pushed herself, to prove she was doing things differently, but she was still holding herself back; her fear of ME returning understandably prevented her from stepping wholeheartedly into the unknown.

Two years later, Amanda received more bad news. Her sister Penny had also become ill with ME: 'To watch someone I love go through it, knowing I couldn't magically fix it, was as hard as going through it myself.' Amanda was compelled to do something positive to inspire her sister, and this gave her fresh motivation: 'If I could prove to my sister that I'd not only recovered, but was stronger than before, she'd have a real-life example of what was possible – proof that she could get through it *and* come out better off.'

The opportunity to do just that presented itself in a text message from a person Amanda used to row with. It read:

'I'm planning to row the Pacific with 2 other girls in an ocean rowing boat in June. We r looking for a 4th girl to join us. Would u like to? . . . Monterey to Hawaii. You'd need to take off from 24 May to end of July – should include a week off in Hawaii at end! What do u reckon?'

The 24th May was in five weeks' time. Knowing it normally takes two years to prepare for an ocean row, Amanda stared at her phone. She felt stunned; not at the text itself, but at the sudden shift within herself: 'I knew I could do this. I had no doubt. I wasn't scared any more. I was just excited. And I knew in that moment I had to do it. I'd been given a second chance!'

She knew from previous adventures that she'd need to be well prepared to succeed, so she planned methodically. She also threw herself into study, gaining five new qualifications in as many weeks: sea survival, yachtmaster theory, first aid, VHF radio licence, advanced ocean navigation. By late May, Amanda was ready, and she boarded a plane to California to join the rest of 'Team Boatylicious'.

As we've seen from her previous adventures, and through her recovery from ME, Amanda had learnt to break down a problem into manageable chunks, and the same was true during this epic rowing journey. With four in the boat and two rowing spaces, Amanda and her crew worked in two-hour shifts. Two would row for two hours before switching to the cabin, where they'd wriggle out of their wet clothing, cook, eat, drink, navigate, check the boat, tend to injuries and sleep – twelve shifts a day; twelve hours of rowing, day and night. 'I'd been told the first twenty-four hours would be the toughest,' Amanda said, 'and that if we could get through that, we could get through the rest. But after twenty-four hours of oars breaking in storms, sea sickness, equipment failure, sleep deprivation and huge waves catching us out in the pitch-black darkness at night, I couldn't imagine braving this for another day, let alone up to seventy!' That's when Amanda made a deal with herself to focus on two hours at a time, rather than think about what lay further ahead. Far better to deal with acute short shifts of stress as they happened than the more chronic stress and worry of thinking about how long she would have to keep up this level of endurance. By adopting this strategy, she was letting her brain handle stress in the way human beings have evolved to handle it: 'I carried on with this plan until I reached Hawaii.'

Amanda reflected on her journey: 'It's amazing how quickly you can react, learn and change when you're continually immersed in difficult situations. In those moments, I was repeatedly faced with a clear choice: give up or fight. And by fight, I mean: try, learn, create, develop, change, find a way somehow – anything it takes to make it work. These were the defining moments that challenged and shaped me the most; where I discovered my best coping strategies.' In this way, her adventures taught Amanda how to respond better to difficulties in everyday life: 'Without the challenges I've come across on my adventures, I wouldn't be as effective at resolving things quickly and confidently in a crisis.'

Despite being incredibly tough, spending two months at sea reminded Amanda how much she enjoyed the simplicity of that kind of lifestyle. 'Physically, it was very demanding, but mentally it was so calming,' she said. 'I felt so alive. Like nothing else mattered. During adventure, all of life's niggling problems, dilemmas and the pressures we put on ourselves in the modern world fade away. Whatever I'm worrying about suddenly seems so small and insignificant in comparison.'

That adventure calms the mind enough to find inner peace (from heartbreak, from tragic loss, from what's been holding you back, from illness and fear) is what each of these stories has in common. That inner calm offers a balm to heal whatever wounds exist. Each of our adventurers found an inner calm in the midst of immense challenge.

And in going on their own personal journeys and achieving their goals, they were able to move forward, just as Amanda went from adventurer to wheelchair-bound to super adventurer. Fifty days after setting off, Amanda entered the *Guinness Book of World Records* as part of the first all-female crew to row across the Pacific Ocean from California to Hawaii. She had recovered and risen, thanks to adventure. 'As we came close to land, I *knew* I'd finally beaten this,' Amanda said. 'The last two months had been the final challenge in a seven-year journey for me. I'd left the ME part of my life behind in California, and I promised myself there and then that I never needed to be scared again.'

We've become friends since that first meeting in Bristol, having shared some small adventures, which is why I'm particularly pleased for Amanda that her sister Penny has now also recovered from ME. The turning point in Penny's recovery was during Amanda's inspiring row. After a year of convalescence, Penny returned to her PhD work part-time and committed to help Team Boatylicious with PR and supporting logistics. Penny wrote to me, 'there was a lot do for the girls and my PhD but eventually I started to feel better and realised I could do more than I thought I could. There was no way I was going to let Amanda down after everything she'd been through, so I just had to get on with it, this was the turning point for me to get better.'

It seems adventure really does boost resilience, reminding us that anything is possible and that we can cope with whatever is thrown our way. And adventure can 'heal', or at least help us with all sorts of mental, physical and behavioural issues. If not a cure-all, it is a particularly good fit as a remedy for our modern maladies. However, I believe adventure should not just be seen as a cure but instead as an element necessary for maximum wellbeing. Rather than applying adventure when there's already a problem, we should knit it into our lives to build better from the beginning. Amanda drew on her childhood adventures in order to recover and to imagine her brighter future. If we want to build stronger resilience, there is possibly no more important time to consider adventure than in our children's lives.

Five

To Grow Up

'I believe we are all explorers at heart – it's part of the human condition. The competitiveness of sport isn't for everyone, but going wild is something that every child can do. By climbing trees and building dens, you become master of your own destiny: you can be an architect, thinker, inventor. You co-operate, you collaborate. As a child, that's incredibly empowering.'

Benedict Allen, explorer

Memories of my own early childhood take me back to the euphoria of discovery. When I was growing up on Alderney in the English Channel, I would leave my house in the morning on my bike and go off exploring all day, either with my best friend or by myself.

I remember the freedom after 'crossing the threshold' as I'd lift my feet from the pedals of my bike and freewheel down the hill to the harbour. I can still remember that feeling of total abandon and fearlessness as I took the bend, down and down. Then that feeling of delightful awe as I pushed back the wrought-iron gate and entered my magical secret place. This is where it all began. This is where I became an explorer.

There I am, eight years old and standing full of wonder in my own special place, a secret garden, full of exotic plants and insects, and what I called the waterfall – a spring with a statue at the far end, hidden from the world. I'd never been to a place so steeped in magic. As a child explorer, I was captivated, and every day for months I would return home to sketch, measure, inspect and record my findings of my secret world. Years later, I found out that the secret garden is a mostly forgotten spring, with a statue of Mary and surrounded by long walls, but it is a real place! I imagined it was just for me, almost never seeing another soul enter.

My secret world was my first foray into exploration and set the stage for all the others that would follow. I'd like to think I've never lost that childlike curiosity to see new places, try new things and to live adventurously. The word 'feral' was frequently used to describe me. But I wasn't alone in my 'feral' nature. The majority of my generation were equally free to explore. Such freedom was the norm.

Those of us born in the 1970s or before will fondly recall, at weekends and during school holidays, our parents sending us off to play after breakfast; we'd only return when we were hungry or before it got dark, whichever came first. We'd modify our landscapes to create our own playgrounds. We'd spend time on our own, lost in our own play, creating imaginary worlds; we'd navigate our way around our locality, finding shortcuts during our explorations, secret pathways we knew were there but adults didn't. Our parents weren't with us to praise or protect us, to remind us to 'be careful' or to stop us from climbing too high or getting too muddy. And we came back in one piece, albeit with shoes scuffed and knees bruised. In fact, I'd argue, we came back with *extra* pieces – of insight about risk-taking and socialising and creating; new pieces of knowledge about playing and surviving and thriving.

Think back to your own childhood. Close your eyes and home in on the most memorable moments. What are the most cherished memories from your childhood? I've asked that question to audiences nationwide, and, notably, if they're thirty years old or older, the happiest childhood memories will almost always be outdoor adventures: climbing trees, kayaking down rivers, exploring on bikes with friends. What about today's kids? What will their memories be? Today, those carefree days of roaming wild feel like a million miles away. Because, these days, the adventures of childhood are, for many, an entirely different experience.

Calls of 'be home by dinner time' have been replaced with 'come off that screen, it's dinner time'. Bruised and scratched skin has been replaced with buying the latest Fortnite skin. Immersion in outdoor activities – building forts and climbing trees – has been replaced with immersion in a pixelated world – building houses in Minecraft. These days, the inner 'call to adventure' which resides deep within us from our hunter-gatherer ancestry is only partially satisfied by gaming in apocalyptic worlds, rather than 'crossing the threshold' in the real one. Modern society keeps kids from doing so. Or if they are allowed to cross it, they mustn't venture too far. Consequently, a vast majority of today's children are restricted – a generation of cotton-wool kids who mustn't walk to school by themselves or climb that too-tall tree. They must hold their parent's hand and 'be careful'.

I wonder now what might have happened to my parents were they to be judged by today's standards. Would I be seen as neglected and be taken away from them? That's what some parents in Maryland state in America were threatened with after trusting their kids (aged ten and six) to walk home alone from the park in 2015. This parental decision led to a visit from the police and Child Protective Services. Lenore Skenazy, president of Let Grow, a nonpartisan, nonprofit organisation promoting childhood independence and resilience, and founder of the Free-Range Kids blog, described the case as a 'hysterical moment in America', as so many parents nowadays seem to 'believe children are in danger every single second they are unsupervised'. And she should know, given the response she received herself when she let her nine-year-old ride the New York subway alone. A couple of days later, Lenore was labelled by *The Today Show* as 'America's worst mum'. Judgemental shaming by news channels aside, this gave Lenore the impetus to start her Free-Range Kids blog, where she explains that although she insists her child wears a helmet and seat belt and follows safety guidelines, she wants to live in a world where loving, rational parents don't get arrested for trusting their kids to do some things without parental supervision.

Is life really more dangerous today than when I was a child? And if that's not the case, why else are children adventuring outdoors and without supervision so much less? A report from Natural England called 'Childhood and Nature: A Survey on Changing Relationships with Nature Across Generations' found that since the 1970s the proportion of children regularly playing in wild places has fallen from over half to fewer than 10 per cent. Alarmingly, according to a poll funded by Persil's Dirt Is Good Campaign, three quarters of kids spend less time outside than prison inmates, with the average child playing freely outside for just four to seven minutes a day. Another survey of 2,000 eight- to twelve-year-olds for the TV channel Eden reported that 64 per cent of British kids play outside less than once a week, 28 per cent haven't been on a country walk in the last year and 20 per cent have never once climbed a tree. No wonder more children are now admitted to British hospitals for injuries from falling out of bed than falling out of trees. And no wonder today's children are heeding their call to adventure by playing video games. They need to become their own heroes somewhere.

As well as this move indoors, the other major change in parenting is the way in which we supervise every moment of our children's time. In a study called 'Urban Children's Access to Their Neighbourhood: Changes Over Three Generations', the author found that since the 1970s the area in which children may roam without supervision has decreased by almost 90 per cent. And a study by the Policy Studies Institute in London found that in 1971 80 per cent of seven- and eight-year-olds walked to school, often alone or with their friends, whereas two decades later fewer than 10 per cent did so – almost all accompanied by their parents. This is how much childhood norms have shifted in a single generation.

Our kids' time, like our own, is under more pressure than it ever has been. We, as parents, expect our children to spend their time as productively as possible, signing them up to after-school clubs and organised sports. This means they have far less opportunity to just shoot the breeze and play freely in their own way and their own time. Add to that the abundance that children now have, with so many toys, TV channels and games to choose from, and, of course, the constant distraction of social media. The opportunity to get bored and lost in their imagination or immersed in wild play has fallen by the wayside. Excess and distraction has replaced boredom, yet it is boredom that cultivates creativity and self-directed learning. In a 2014 study entitled 'Does Being Bored Make Us More Creative?', Sandi Mann and Rebekah Cadman tested participants' divergent thinking ability, their capacity to 'think outside the box', by measuring their aptitude to invent multiple uses for items or to make connections between seemingly unrelated ideas. Before the tests, some of the subjects were asked to copy names from a phonebook. The bored phonebook-copying group scored higher in divergent thinking than the control group who did not have to copy names. Researchers believe that boredom might lead to an openness to, and willingness for, new ideas.

As well as a drive for productivity, echoing our own pressured lives, the other reason for oversupervising our kids has to be a rise in parental fear. For a 2004 book *Public Space and the Culture of Childhood*, seventy parents of children aged eight to eleven were interviewed. The vast majority considered that today's kids were at greater risk than their forbears. Some fears are justified – for example, the amount of traffic on the roads has increased exponentially. However, it can be difficult to judge the severity of the threats. We have more information available to us than ever before, and social media and newspaper headlines can give us an unrealistic view of the world. The impression we may have that 'stranger danger' has increased in recent decades is likely due to its coverage in the media rather than the facts. According to Home Office statistics published in January 2010, the odds of a child being abducted by a stranger in the United Kingdom remains the same as thirty years ago: one in a million.

And now there's also the fear of litigation. Institutions don't want to be sued, so they err on the side of caution and overprotect. This leads them to 'restrict and prevent rather than empower and enable,' says Rob Wheway, a leading children's play consultant who has worked in play for more than thirty-five years, carrying out safety inspections and assessments for seventeen of those. He thinks it's not so much that we're an increasingly risk-averse society – many parents he's consulted with want their children to experience the freedom they had – rather it's standards being imposed or the misinterpretation of those safety standards which removes the risk. In his report 'Not a Risk-Averse Society', Rob says 'a culture of risk aversion is being imposed by those responsible for the Health and Safety of the general public' thanks to 'over-cautious interpretations of guidance'. Rob's report recommends 'those with responsibilities for Health and Safety need to avoid control measures which have a detrimental effect on health which is out of all proportion to any increases in safety'. It seems the Health and Safety Executive, Britain's national regulator for workplace health and safety, agrees: 'Exposure to well managed risks helps children learn important life skills, including how to manage risks for themselves ... children, in particular need to learn how to manage risks, and adventure activities such as rock climbing, sailing and canoeing are an ideal way of doing this.' Even safety crusaders understand that reasonable risks are essential for our children's healthy development, but the fear of litigation means that in practice these guidelines are pushed aside in preference of caution.

It's interesting that there is this friction between what we are actually doing and what we know, instinctively, is right – that as parents we want the same freedom for our children as we had, and that safety organisations recognise the importance of risk for development. And yet we are still overprotecting.

We're already seeing remarkable evidence that our young adults seem to be struggling to cope with everyday problems. One university counselling service has reported that students are increasingly seeking help (even calling the police) after such minor incidences as seeing a mouse in their apartment or being called a name by a fellow student. These are not atypical examples. Mental ill health and low adaptive functioning within new university student populations has been reported to be problematically high in numerous research studies and in multiple countries. Students arrive without the coping mechanisms to deal with day-to-day living, let alone the pressure and challenges of study. But there is another way.

Adventurous play is about learning how to fall, dust yourself off and get up again. As we learnt in the previous chapter, it's about developing resilience. It's surely better for children to learn how to cope with obstacles and challenges while they're young than to enter adulthood ill-equipped to cope, out of their depth and with nobody to help them. Adventure gives children the opportunity to be challenged, to overcome obstacles and to gain those important coping skills that will set them in good stead for life. As such, developing coping mechanisms is a huge part of the Adventure Effect for kids. It's also about learning how to manage risk and take responsibility for yourself.

In his book *No Fear: Growing Up in a Risk Averse Society*, Tim Gill, who used to advise the British government on children's play and was the director of the Children's Play Council for six years, argues that children who are granted the opportunity to assess and deal with risks in play can learn important life skills and experience for the real world. It is a stance that is supported by the anthropologists Pia Christensen and Miguel Romero Mikkelsen, who found that the Danish children they studied, aged ten to twelve, demonstrated the ability to evaluate risks, while simultaneously assessing their personal physical abilities and limits. They argue that risk engagement is a necessary process that allows children to develop awareness of their particular limitations and learn from their own mistakes.

What if we let our children gradually take on responsibilities, giving them the chance to feel competent and independent and to master risk-taking for themselves? That's precisely what happens at The Yard, which opened in 2016.

The Yard is a 50,000 square foot 'junk playground' on Governors Island in New York Harbor, open to six- to thirteen-year-olds. There are no shiny plastic slides or super-safe seesaws, no baby-sized bucket swings. Stacks of pallets and tyres provide the perfect den-building materials, and filthy mattresses become makeshift trampolines. Nails, hammers, saws and crowbars lie around the site. A fifteen-foot platform acts as a climbing frame. The Yard has a free and permissive atmosphere with few rules: no phones or electronic devices, no flip-flops and no adults. It is staffed by professionally trained playworkers who keep a close eye on the kids but don't intervene all that much.

There are roughly 1,000 'junk playgrounds' worldwide. Every aspect needs to pass a complicated risk-benefit assessment, but the underlying ethos is that children have a natural sense of self-preservation like we all do. Here, they are able to weigh up danger and test it out for themselves. The kids learn by doing, which is always the best and most memorable way to learn. The most fascinating part of this is that relaxing the rigid rules doesn't make children less safe or more unruly, but it does make them more engaged, resourceful and independent. Bruises and scratches are common, but in the four years since they've opened there's never been a serious injury at The Yard. Similar safety outcomes are recorded at the other sites.

'I came to the counterintuitive conclusion that engaging in risk is actually very important in preventing injuries,' says Mariana Brussoni, a researcher with the Child and Family Research Institute in Vancouver, who conducted a review of the studies on playground safety in 2015. She found that children learn how their bodies and the world works, and that these fundamental skills ultimately protect them.

Like anything in life, we get better with practice; the more risks we take, the better we get at risk-taking, and, most importantly, the better we get at assessing and mitigating risk and knowing what to do in uncertain and challenging situations. Most, if not all, important aspects of life come with some risk. Experience of risk assessment allows us to understand and analyse these situations more accurately and move forward with confidence. So, learning to assess risk effectively opens doors to possibilities throughout life, because life is challenging and filled with uncertainty. We can't know exactly what will happen in the future. What we can do, though, is equip ourselves better to cope with uncertainty, challenge and adversity.

Experienced adventurers take responsibility for their actions and do everything in their power to reduce the chance of injury. Consequently, they are less likely to hurt themselves when faced with danger or risky situations. The opposite is often true of those who've been protected from taking any kind of risk. Rather than protecting us, becoming unaccustomed to dealing with risk makes us less equipped to cope with the inevitable challenges of life.

As naturalist and author Stephen Moss says, cotton-wool kids are missing out on 'learning how to take responsibility for yourself, and how – crucially – to measure risk for yourself. Falling out of a tree is a very good lesson in risk and reward.' Youngsters who've learnt to manage risks for themselves and make informed decisions as a result are *safer* than those who have never been exposed to risk. How ironic that those given the freedom to take risks and rise to challenges end up safer than those wrapped in cotton wool and prevented from doing so.

As well as being 'good' for our children's resilience and autonomy, there is real joy to be found in freedom and adventurous play too. If we remove some of the rules and restrictions from children's playtime and add more challenge, as was the case in a two-year experiment conducted in New Zealand in 2017, maybe we'd reveal happier kids as well. In the trial, eight schools increased opportunities for risk and challenge (such as rough-and-tumble play), reduced rules and added loose equipment to their play environment. Teachers worried that chaos would ensue, but what happened was the complete opposite – this no-rules experiment resulted in fewer reports of bullying and the children being happier and more sociable.

So, what if we considered relaxing some of our rules? And what if we just let our children explore with childlike wonder like we used to? Following my three-year-old son on even the simplest of walks in a new place it becomes clear to me that it is an adventure to him. He sees the world through a lens of boundless energy and opportunity. We often don't move further than a few hundred metres in an hour because he sees and appreciates the variety and uniqueness surrounding him and he wants to explore it. Modern life drags us from nature and pushes us to conform and follow rules. The two pressures eventually dampen the spirit, so much so that the excitement, wonder and adventure of the world around us is often hidden from the gaze of most adults. What if we became more curious about exploring the wonders of our own world, like our children naturally are? And what if we allowed our children to follow their inbuilt curiosity as they grow?

I have spent my life learning how to challenge myself, assess and take risks on my own terms, to push my boundaries and do more than I thought I could do. I have reaped the benefits of taking those risks and facing those challenges. As a parent, I feel I'm obligated to raise my son to be able to deal with future adversities and challenges, to be resilient and independent. But I also understand the acute fear and worry we have as parents who love our children dearly and have an innate desire to protect them from danger. I, too, am deeply affected by the stories of children injured or worse; it's impossible not to feel a sense of injustice and grief when any child is harmed. My job is to keep my son safe, but it's also to prepare him for the world. I am torn between what I know is best for him and wanting to wrap him in cotton wool. When should I allow my son the autonomy to make his own decisions and take his own risks: to climb a tree, to play out of my sight even if for just fifteen minutes? One day I want him to go off for an adventure on his bicycle, to explore the fields around our house on his own, as I once did, but just thinking about it worries me.

I don't know all the answers, but I believe the solution is in balance, just as we need to find a balance of mental health and safety across the whole of our community. Every child is different, so there's not one way of parenting. But armed with the knowledge that challenge and adversity are important, as well as acknowledging the impulse to protect, maybe as parents and communities we can find a better balance? A balance between supervised and out-of-sight activities as children get older and push for a little more independence; between indoors and outdoors; between adventure time and screen time.

If children can have their own adventures, make their own mistakes, take their own risks when ready, I'm certain they are far more likely to grow into healthy, happy, capable adults who'll flourish. And I'd argue there is possibly no more important time than when we move from being children to adults.

The hero's journey isn't just for books and movies; it is a journey each of us goes on as we 'cross the threshold' from childhood into adulthood – a time away from normal routines that starts with letting go of what you were, followed by a transition period when you find something new in yourself as you explore, and the final stage of bringing the lessons home as you find a meaningful role in the world.

For our ancestors, these transitions were marked with a ceremony or ritual. An individual would leave childhood and enter adulthood. These rites of passage gave youths a chance to prove their new status in the community and to themselves. As such, they were characterised by ordeal, risk, responsibility, fresh perspective and pride. Examples include the young men of the Pentecost Island, Vanuatu, who would jump from tall towers between twenty and thirty metres high with only vines strapped to their legs, or the Maasai of East Africa who would hunt their first lion.

Today, challenging rites of passage are no longer the norm. But researchers and youth practitioners have seen that without community-sanctioned rites of passage, young people create them for themselves, such as gang membership, drug and alcohol use, or bullying. Risk-taking and novelty-seeking are hallmarks of typical adolescent behaviour. It's believed that this is because the self-monitoring and decision-making part of the brain – the prefrontal cortex – is still developing in the teenage years. That and the fluctuating hormones thought to contribute to impulsive behaviours. Such behaviours can aid the development of independence, but they can also render the adolescent more vulnerable to harm. Indeed, the risk of injury or death is higher during the adolescent period than in adulthood or childhood. And when you take into account that roughly half of all lifetime mental disorders start by our mid-teens and three quarters by our mid-twenties, it raises questions about how we can support our young people's journeys into adulthood.

Just as releasing the reigns is important for younger children to allow them to experience real or apparent risk, so too is harnessing the desire in older children to take risks by presenting them with opportunities to pursue healthy adventures rather than unhealthy ones. This desire could be satisfied by going on life- and self-defining immersive adventures.

In 2016, at my annual adventure gathering Base Camp Festival, big-wall climber and mountaineer Andy Kirkpatrick told me how he guided his thirteen-year-old-daughter Ella to climb Yosemite's El Capitan. El Cap, as it's known amongst climbers, is a 3,000-feet vertical rock face of sheer granite – that's the height of six London Eyes stacked on top of each other. The climbing is arduous.

'Climbing and the rewards and risks of that life make me who I am, and the lessons it has taught me are lessons I've tried to pass on to my kids,' Andy told me. 'Adventure is in my DNA, and so it's in theirs also.' Although he never felt certain whether having them tag along with him when he talked about his adventures was a good idea or not, it meant they got to see what he got up to when he went away, and they could understand both the risks and rewards of striving for impossible things. Rather than pushing his children into climbing, Andy said he wanted to 'leave it up to them to decide how to explore the boundaries of themselves. Exposing them to wilderness and danger the way my dad did, giving the impression of both while keeping them on a short leash.'

Climbing El Cap had become Ella's goal, so Andy made it happen. Andy had climbed El Cap thirty times, once in eighteen hours, and had spent 'almost two months hanging from it' in total, so if anyone knew how to keep his daughter safe, he did. They trained hard, and Ella learnt how to pass knots, and about wall safety, aiding and self-rescue.

They arrived in Yosemite in 2012 ready for four days of climbing and living on the wall. Despite the unprecedented heat, Ella started well, her enthusiasm pushing her on. But during the second day, she became increasingly tired, getting slower and slower. That night she was so tired her dad had to take her shoes off and put her into her sleeping bag, 'seeing in her the heavy fatigue that only a wall can bring'. On the third day, Ella struggled, her exhaustion and tears visible as she reached the end of her tether. But when her dad shouted up to the other teammates that they might need to haul her up the next two pitches as she was too tired, Ella came round: 'She shouted, "No! I want to do it myself. If I don't, I'll only be disappointed."' And with that, she slowly made her way up two more rope lengths. 'To say I was stunned by her strength, grit and determination would be an understatement. I knew it was this show of will that I had wanted to mine all along, the inner strength that she had − and we all have − but even so, I had to find my strength not to cry.'

For four hard days and nights, Ella climbed the vertical rock face and made it to the top herself. Andy saw his daughter change: 'At the beginning of the climb, I tied onto the rope with my young child, a human I helped to create, under my protection, the pieces of her still to be ordered, someone I loved. As we got higher, and she did not fold or crumble, and grasped that she was as strong as the rest of us, sometimes stronger, I lost that child, but there before me, on that summit, stood a young woman bold enough to know she had nothing to fear.'

And herein lies the key to why adventure is so important to both children and adults: through adventure, we discover an inner strength we didn't know we had. Through rising to challenges and overcoming obstacles, we show ourselves that we can do and be more than we thought. Imagine going through life without knowing what you were truly capable of. Imagine going through life without ever uncovering this inner strength. That is the cost of not allowing our children to adventure. Step by step, we need to believe in our children and trust them. Only then will they learn to believe in themselves.

Six

To Face Fear

'Ships in harbour are safe, but that's not what ships are built for.'

John Shedd, author

Standing on a slab of rock, a few metres above the Zambezi River, Richie squeezed into his life jacket. As I watched, I remember thinking that they aren't really designed for him – a man born without arms. Our expedition leader Ken had asked him and the rest of his team to jump into the treacherous river. Until that point, Richie had never considered his disability a disadvantage. 'It looks worse than it is. It's just normal to me,' he'd say. But right then Richie was about to plunge into the furious waters to reach a raft manned by one of the expert kayakers helping the expedition. 'As an adult, I've never jumped into water, not even a swimming pool,' admitted a frightened Richie, who waited at the back, having opted to go last.

From the raft, we would run the Zambezi River, navigating the rapids using teamwork to avoid capsizing and being thrown into the churning water. The danger from drowning or severe injury is real; the movement and intensity of the water is unpredictable – you could be held under or smashed against rocks.

I wasn't just concerned for Richie on this second *Beyond Boundaries* trip. The whole team faced challenges, from Kate who was partially paralysed to Heidi who was fully paralysed below the waist.

Below Richie, the river waited, bubbling white and roaring impatiently. 'I was worrying about how the life jacket might slip off and I'd be lost. It was terrifying,' Richie said. 'That happened to me when I was a kid. I jumped in the sea and the life jacket flew off. That gave me my fear of water.' His body must have been in overload. Just watching him on the rock, my heart was pounding.

Zambezi River white-water rafting has been classified by the British Canoe Union as 'extremely difficult – long and violent rapids with severe hazards. Continuous, powerful, confused water'. The river has taken 300 million years to cut the basalt gorge below the Victoria Falls, which somehow adds to its drama and intensity. Once you enter, there is really only one way to go: down the river.

The first time I rafted the Zambezi I was a fearless and foolhardy nineteen-year-old. I would join the rafting guides on their days off to 'test drive' new sections of the river. Now I was back with the BBC to record the second *Beyond Boundaries* expedition of people with disabilities, this time across Africa. After a decade of going on expeditions and seeing people damaged and worse, my youthful, carefree approach had been replaced with a predisposition to consider all the what-ifs. At nineteen, you think you're indestructible. But life erodes that certainty until it is the *acceptance* of risk and danger rather than the *ignorance* of it that allows you to take on these challenges as a savvier yet less fearless adventurer.

Working out a risk-assessment to send a team of people with different specific challenges – from blindness and deaf-ness to amputees and wheelchair users – down a rapid of this magnitude was, however, terrifying. We had the best rafting guides in the world, but the facts remained: Richie had no arms, Mark was deaf, and Kate and Heidi didn't have the use of their legs. I was in a state of heightened alertness and stress. But Richie, well he was being thrown in at the deep end, quite literally.

I spoke to Richie in 2020 to catch up and find out how he remembered the expedition. 'As we approached the falls, the incredible sound of it hit me,' Richie said. 'That rumble. And the vapour rising in the air added to the drama, which was already intense. It was a shock to be asked to jump in. I was petrified. I was doing those big gulps like you see in cartoons.' Richie remembered watching the others from his team jump in one by one, their heads disap-pearing under the white foam: 'The others seemed to stay under the water for ages.' Finally, it was Richie's turn, and he knew he had to do it. Earlier decisions had brought him to this point of no return. Now that it mattered and others were counting on him, there was no turning back. He had one final glance over the side of the rock, took a deep breath and jumped in.

Richie remembers being underwater 'an awful long time'. Eventually, his yellow helmet briefly appeared in the foam before being swept downriver: 'I was relieved, and, luckily, the jacket stayed on, as the team had put straps on it under my legs. It was a bit Heath Robinson, but it worked.' Richie made it to the kayak, beaming, and the kayak took him to the raft. The porter team clapped and cheered from the sides of the gorge, and the collective sense of relief amongst the leadership team was palpable. But it was not over yet. There was still seven miles of canyon and twenty rapids to run. Richie was silent in the raft, taking it all in.

The most violent rapid on the river was the fourth, but Richie's team kept it together and made it through without tipping. Another deep sigh of relief, but it lasted only a few seconds before the wild rodeo ride continued, the raft being thrown around like a sock in a washing machine. Having survived the most notorious rapid, Richie was now in high spirits. 'The feeling is exhilarating!' Richie exclaimed from his raft.

Meanwhile, the team in the other raft weren't so lucky. They flipped at the fourth rapid, and all of them ended up in the raging river, with Sophie, who was born with dwarfism, being dragged all the way into the next rapid. She was finally pulled out to safety by a kayak positioned at the end of the fifth rapid and hoisted back into the raft. 'I didn't think it would be like that!' cried Sophie. 'It just hits you. You've got no time to think about it. You just go whoosh!' Then she laughed to cheers of encouragement.

Looking back Richie understood that the whole *Beyond Boundaries* experience made him braver. Having endured oppressive heat, unforgiving swamps and the extreme white waters of the African wilderness, the experience proved to him that he could do more than he thought he could and gave him a better understanding of people. 'It also gave me a deeper sense of adventure,' said Richie, who was proud to show his children footage of him doing something spectacular. 'I've gotten braver since I went to Africa, because I realised if I can do that, then I can do anything. The more you do, the more you try and the more you feel you can do.' Richie has since bought a boat and often goes sailing on a whim with friends.

'The rafting was brilliant,' he recalled. 'I loved going down the rapids. I was petrified about turning over at any moment, but I still loved it. Now it's the same with sailing in rough seas. I love riding the biggest waves, although I don't choose to go in the water if I can help it.'

Although he didn't feel it at the time, Richie now recognised that throwing himself into one of the most dangerous rivers in the world had another benefit: 'It helped me a little bit with my fear of water. I've not jumped into water voluntarily since, but I know that if I fall in now, I'll be all right, and if I have to do it, I can. For example, I know if someone was drowning, I could find the strength to jump in, because I've done it and survived.'

Reflecting on the whole experience, Richie said, 'I discovered that adventure makes you feel alive.' Indeed, what's notable about Richie's story and others featuring people who've felt the fear and done it anyway is that the fear turned into joy. Only when we unpick what fear actually is can we begin to see why that is and, in doing so, respond well to the fears we face.

What is fear?

'There is freedom waiting for you, on the breezes of the sky. And you ask, "What if I fall?" Oh, but my darling, "What if you fly?"'

'What if you fly?', Erin Hanson

Fear is an important part of being human. It is evolutionarily useful to be afraid. Being fearless increases the likelihood of harm – animals learn (often the hard way) that they must run from predators. It's the same with humans. Young children are naturally brave and constantly pushing boundaries, stepping outside of their comfort zones on a daily basis. We need to be taught about the dangers around us and learn to be concerned and fearful enough to protect ourselves from those dangers.

Take busy roads. Toddlers would happily run into a busy road before they are taught about the dangers and before they can compute the fact that if hit by a moving car, they wouldn't survive. It's only once we know the risk of being hit by a car that we use this fear for our benefit and survival. This kind of fear is useful because it stops us from stepping out in front of a moving vehicle.

Being fearful is a protective measure because it enables you to assess risk and take precautions; for example, to make sure there are plenty of experts in kayaks on the river ready and able to rescue the *Beyond Boundaries* explorers if necessary. Fear ensures you consider worst-case scenarios and prepare accordingly.

As we learnt in chapter three, millions of years of evolution have honed our fight-or-flight response to stress or threat. This response is hardwired into the human psyche and was an evolutionary advantage, allowing us to survive in a harsh, unpredictable world. Today, when our brain's fear centre is alerted, our innate response prepares and equips us to respond to danger so that we have the best possible chance of survival. That's how fear informs and protects us.

When Richie stood on the rock looking down at the boiling river, before his conscious mind could unravel the information in front of him, his eyes relayed the sight to his brain for evaluation: is this a potential threat? When he sensed danger, the fear centre of the brain (the amygdala) automatically sent a distress signal to the control centre (the hypothalamus), which told his adrenal gland to start pumping the stress hormone adrenaline into his bloodstream. Adrenaline dilated the bronchial tubes in his lungs to make space for more air and increased Richie's breathing. It made his heart beat faster so the oxygen-laden blood flowed more rapidly to his brain to sharpen his senses and to his muscles to prepare them to flee or fight. Adrenaline also triggered the release of more glucose into the bloodstream, giving his body a quick energy boost to respond immediately to the danger.

Meanwhile, the neurotransmitter noradrenaline spurted from the nerve endings of his sympathetic nervous system. It triggered the narrowing of his blood vessels, which increased his blood pressure and ultimately acted to increase the force of his muscle contractions. The veins in his skin constricted to send more blood to major muscle groups and was responsible for the fearful chill Richie felt, because there was suddenly less blood in the skin to keep it warm.

Once the initial surge of adrenaline started to subside, the hypothalamus activated the second stage of Richie's fear response, the adrenal-cortical system. His pituitary gland secreted ACTH (adrenocorticotropic hormone), which moved through the bloodstream to the adrenal cortex, where it activated the release of approximately thirty different hormones, including cortisol, that kept his body revved up and on high alert. His entire body was neurologically hijacked by these floods of neurochemicals, but it was hijacked for his own benefit – to redirect energy and to sharpen his senses.

This automatic process, triggered by a distress message, can make us faster and stronger than normal, all helpful when you are about to navigate a raging river or run from a predator. Vladimir Zatsiorsky, a professor of kinesiology at Penn State University, has studied the biomechanics of weightlifting. He defines 'absolute strength' as the force our muscles are theoretically able to apply and 'maximal strength' as the maximum force they can generate through the conscious exertion of will. He found that trained weightlifters summoned around 80 per cent of their absolute strength in training sessions whereas the rest of us can usually only summon about 65 per cent. The stress of competition elicited the fight or flight response and a rush of adrenaline which allowed the experienced weightlifters to access even more of their strength, as much as 92 per cent. There's evidence to suggest that the more intense the competition, the more power the athletes can access, as their innate fear response boosts performance. As Jeff Wise, author of *Extreme Fear*, notes, 'It's no coincidence that world records in athletic events tend to get broken at major events like the Olympics, where the stakes are highest and the pressure is the greatest.' This is how the fear process prepares us and optimises us for prime performance.

Fear is a good thing, because it prepares us, but it also offers us valuable information. This has been found to be especially striking in participants in extreme sport. 'Fear becomes information, not something to hold you back,' said Dr Eric Brymer at the Adventure Mind conference in 2020. Dr Brymer has spent years at the Australian College of Applied Psychology and the Leeds Beckett University studying the psychology of extreme athletes like big-wave surfers, white-water kayakers and BASE jumpers. He explained that feeling fear means 'take this seriously, do your homework, get trained'; it's an input that leads to a more in-depth assessment. That assessment might elicit further preparation, or the decision to wait for another day, or the choice to go for it, but the response is based on information rather than recklessness; the decision to not go for it is informed by deliberation rather than instinctual fear.

Fear can be less useful when it stops us from acting when we would benefit from doing so. We can instead become overwhelmed, paralysed. For example, Richie could have let his fear of water stop him from jumping. He would've then returned home feeling jaded and disappointed rather than elated and motivated.

We experience fear when facing real situations in the moment and anxiety when we consider what *might* happen in the future, whether that's the possibility of pain, the danger of death or the embarrassment of what others might think. Both fear and anxiety elicit the fight or flight response so both can make us freeze. We worry how others might judge us, and it stops us from creating art or speaking publicly. Because what if they hate it? Our fear of failure stops us from trying. Because what if I lose my job and security? Our fear of discomfort or pain stops us from adventuring. Because what if I get cold and wet or fall and hurt myself?

But what if, instead of letting fear sit in the driving seat, we listen to what fear is saying, thank it for alerting us to danger and preparing us in readiness, then politely tell it to move into the backseat so that we can take control of our lives? What if we create, we try and we adventure instead? Sometimes the fear won't go away, so you have to continue, afraid.

Richie's fear was 'What if I slip through the life jacket or get flipped into the water and drown?' But Richie didn't let his fear take control and stop him from jumping. He was terrified – with good reason – but he still did the thing that scared him. Even though his flight or fight instinct had sensed the threat and engaged his emotional brain and supercharged his senses in preparation, he didn't run away; he jumped right into that swirling, raging river. Richie switched from seeing what was frightening him as a threat and reframed it as a challenge. His logical mind reminded him how far he'd come; that he couldn't let people down; that this was a challenge he needed to rise to.

We can all do this too, but first we need to understand how fear relates to bravery. Because the opposite of fear is not courage. Brave people still feel fear. The difference between courage and fear is that courage is a choice, fear isn't. Fear is an evolutionary response to danger, an automatic instinct that is inbuilt to protect us. Bravery is about acting *despite* perceived risk or danger or uncertainty. That might be the physical danger of drowning in the rapids or the social danger of drowning in a pool of other people's criticism or simply the danger of not knowing what will happen, where the outcome is uncertain. Brave people are not fearless. Fear is an essential part of being brave. So how do we actively choose to feel the fear and do it anyway?

How can we learn to be brave?

I will always remember when fear took hold of me as I stood waiting my turn to jump off the bridge linking Zimbabwe and Zambia. I was nineteen years old, on my earliest adventure in Africa, and it was the first time I'd heard the thunder of Victoria Falls and the Zambezi River below. I heard what pure fear sounds like on that bridge – a primal wrench of a scream as, one by one, people bungee jumped down a 111-metre drop, legs tied together. It was the sound of a wild animal, a groan forced out of the body involuntarily, like nothing else I've ever heard before or since coming from a human being. It wasn't attractive. Not everyone moaned but a good proportion did, and I remember resolving that I wouldn't make that sound myself. Soon it was my turn to jump. As I walked to the platform, my body flooded with adrenaline. My hands were clammy, my heart was pounding and, even though I'd been reminded by the instructor to look forward and out rather than down, all I felt was 100 per cent pure fear. I listened to his instructions in a haze and then the countdown began. The moment just before I pushed off was, to this day, the most scared I've ever been. There is something in our DNA that tells us *not* to jump off high objects; every part of my body was screaming at me to stop.

Yet the moment after I jumped was serene. As I pushed out into thin air, my eyes looking forwards along the river gorge, the fear dissolved almost immediately and morphed into exhilaration. I screamed a whooping bellow of victory as I gently fell. (I may also have made that guttural animal call the moment I pushed off too – I'll never know.) It felt like it lasted minutes, though in reality it was just seconds. All of the worry about what could go wrong – the cord snapping, the crocodiles in the river below me or hitting concrete-like water at the bottom – simply vanished. The actual 'doing' was a gift. I felt alive. I felt a massive rush of relief and happiness; a huge grin spread across my face. The anticipation and the moment of facing the fear head-on had been the hard part; once I'd overcome that fear, the falling was graceful, peaceful, joyful. I was elated.

When we notice a potential threat, our bodies respond and we feel scared. This happens automatically, and the best way we can reduce its hold over us is by moving from the feeling part of our brain to the thinking part. If you can distract your mind from the situation that is causing fear, you'll be better able to behave bravely. For example, world-champion cliff diver Gary Hunt juggles before he jumps off. Experts also recommend counting as a way to distract our brain from getting wrapped up in fearful thoughts. Our brain can only focus on one thought process at once, so if you occupy it with a cognitive task like counting, it can concentrate on that rather than what is in front of it. It is a useful tool that can help you regain control over your thinking if you feel you are being paralysed into inaction by fear. I can remember the counting before I pushed off the bridge above the Zambezi with extraordinary clarity. I must have focused all my attention on it and away from the fear itself. It worked: it was time to jump before I had realised, so I just did it.

Another useful tactic is to take our thoughts to court. Rather than concentrating on possible negative outcomes (like the bungee cord snapping), instead focus on what you know to be the factual truth about the situation (I had watched a dozen people go before me and the cord hadn't snapped). Knowledge can give our confidence a boost by providing evidence to dispute judgemental thoughts. For example, reminding yourself that there are enough highly trained people around who can instantly respond if you get into danger can help quell unhelpful thoughts, as can focusing on facts about an activity that you've trained hard for. Remind yourself of your own capabilities and that risks and eventualities have been well considered and sufficiently prepared for. It is also worth noting that the actual likelihood of death while bungee jumping is one in 500,000, compared to the risk of death while on a car journey, which is one in 20,000.

To help us be brave, we can also choose to change our point of view about a situation – the facts about whatever is causing us to feel fearful remain the same, but a deliberate shift is made in how we see it. One way is to pretend you're excited rather than scared: the two emotions present us with similar physical symptoms, but one may be easier to manage in the moment. Our brains don't know the difference, and faking it until we make it can work well. Another tactic is to reframe fear itself as a help rather than a hindrance, to see the physical fight-or-flight response as a route towards optimal performance. I have used my knowledge of how fear works, and the knowledge of how I've previously experienced fear in dangerous situations, to perceive it as though it were a superpower, because if you think about it, it kind of is: it can make you lightning fast, have supersonic hearing and be as strong as a superhero.

These methods for hacking our fear don't just work on adventures: they carry over into everyday situations like public speaking. Because of my passion for sharing the benefits of adventure and my keenness to start an adventure revolution, I've taken up giving talks. I was awful when I started and petrified. You might think, What's the worst that could happen? Well, my first public talk was so bad I actually fell off the stage! The worst happened. But, in a way, it was a blessing in disguise, because I survived. It was embarrassing, but I was OK. I knew that to share my message I'd have to keep speaking, and I also knew it couldn't get much worse. Thankfully, over time I've improved (at least, I've not fallen off a stage again), but I've never lost that fear.

I still feel the fear, but because of my years of adventure, I've been able to frame it as useful – my superpower – and keep going. I know the fear helps to keep me on my toes. In this way, my fear of public speaking keeps me engaged and helps me perform. I reframe that feeling as I walk out on stage to give a presentation as my source of power. I am still terrified of talking in public, but I know it will give me a boost, so I embrace the fear in that context and carry on.

I have friends who have equally valid things to say, but their fear stops them from getting on the stage. The difference is how we each perceive fear – as something helpful to equip us, or as something to stop us. For me, it's preparation. For them, it's prevention. For those people, just the thought of public speaking and the accompanying anxious feelings have created mental 'stop' signs that prevent them from taking the bold action.

One of the most important examples of reframing is to redefine threats as challenges, even opportunities, like Richie did. The notion of a threat is demoralising and overwhelming, but a challenge or opportunity is enlivening. Consider the following scenario: following days of rain, you return home to find the ground floor flooded. Your housemate is frantically rushing around swearing and picking things up, only to drop them again in the rising water. His face is getting redder as the water rises higher. He's struggling to think straight or breathe. On the other hand, although you feel your heart rate speed up, you take a deep breath and think. You need to get rid of the water coming in as fast as it rises. Another inhale and exhale and you come up with a plan of action. You tell your housemate to go outside and take some deep breaths and suggest he slowly moves the most valuable things upstairs while you drive to B&Q to get a portable pump. Back home, you attach a hose to the pump, and as the water flows out of the house into the street, you breathe a sigh of relief and head back inside to make a cup of tea and help your housemate assess the damage. Same situation, two different responses. One person was caught up in the threat of the situation and his fear prevented him from thinking clearly and taking bold action. Meanwhile, you saw the threat as a challenge and were able to gain clarity and act accordingly.

How we respond in a crisis has a lot to do with whether we see something as a challenge or a threat. And that perception has a lot to do with what kind of thoughts we've repeated to ourselves in the past, for it is those types of thoughts that become our own mental schemas and beliefs. People who tend to have a lot of anxious 'what if' or depressive 'judgemental' thoughts are more likely to see stressors as threats, while people who don't regularly worry about the future or ruminate on the past quite as much may see the same stressors as challenges. I believe adventure can help you rewire your brain for crisis situations, so they appear to you as difficult challenges, not overwhelming threats. This is why the more people go on adventures, the more evidence they have to dispute any previous thoughts they might have had that said, 'I can't do this.' They've proven that they can. In particular, they have faced fear. Living adventurously sets up feedback that helps people see obstacles (or life itself) as a series of challenges that are possible to overcome rather than threats that are impossible to deal with. By living adventurously, we can reprogram ourselves to see challenges and opportunities rather than threats, because we repeatedly prove that we can rise to those challenges, overcome obstacles and emerge the other side, triumphant.

This is one of the most important mindsets the Adventure Effect has given me. If you react to difficulties and emergencies in life as challenges and opportunities, you empower yourself to engage and try, rather than freeze or give up. You become emboldened in life; you have a secret superpower.

The adventure of facing fear

Seeing fear itself as an adventure – as a mountain to climb; as a quest to go on – is how Paula McGuire went from feeling so scared at the thought of joining a four-person book group that she blacked out to standing in front of an audience of 600 giving a TEDx talk about how 'adventure isn't out there ... it's in here', pointing to her head.

In June 2017, adventurer Alastair Humphreys suggested Paula contact me for help; she was about to take on a long-distance swimming challenge and needed a support crew. In her introductory email, she described herself as 'a recluse turned adventurer, who used adventure to overcome debilitating social anxiety and depression'. As well as helping find her adventure teammates, I listened to her story and was intrigued by her bravery. We finally met when she came to share her story at my adventure festival later that year.

For twenty years, Paula had battled with her nerves, and they had won every time. She told me, 'When you struggle to leave your house, and answering a phone is one stress too far, you withdraw from life, like sunshine from a daytrip. Fighting my way back out taught me the benefit of treating every challenge as an adventure and making even the mundane momentous.' Paula had tried everything. She'd been on medication, tried counselling, hypnotherapy, but all had failed to cure her neuroses. So, she 'learnt to stop looking outside of myself for solutions to problems on the inside'.

In 2012, Paula decided that adventure would be her therapy, and ever since she has 'terrified herself daily in the name of recovery. So far it's working.'

Paula, who claims to be the 'world's least likely adventurer', faced her fears in deep water, a snow hole, a haunted house, on a skeleton run, a high dive and that iconic red TEDx carpet. She decided that barriers were only barriers if you stopped at them. Hers, since childhood, had been her fears and anxieties, and fed up with not being able to find a way around them, she decided the only way was to climb over them instead – to face the things that scared her the most and deal with the consequences: 'My nerves suddenly became the thing to stand upon, my very own jungle gym. I was forever scared, nay, terrified of people, of what they thought of me, how they judged my tics. TEDx gave me the opportunity to do that en masse, and it felt bloody good. Fear, when used well, is a remarkable motivator. Standing on that iconic circle of red carpet was just as scary as I had imagined it would be, but that only meant it could be my biggest adventure yet.'

Paula found that the sense of adventure doesn't only exist in outdoor challenges: 'It's something in you, that you choose to take with you or choose to leave behind. Adventure is in my pocket now, and off we jolly well go.

'Protecting myself from fear for twenty years kept me in a box of my own making, living life to the emptiest and pretending I had everything I needed in there. Nowadays, I welcome fear, encourage it even, egging myself on to the point at which the nerves kick back in, then finding new ways to cope. And it's good for me. Being scared by the big things reminds me not to be scared by the little.'

Paula had tried a life where fear dictated her behaviour and prevented her from living, and it hadn't worked out for her. So, she decided to reimagine how she felt about and experienced being afraid. By choosing to embrace fear, she empowered herself and discovered that life is meant to be lived not feared.

Seven

To Stretch and Grow

'Only those who will risk going too far can possibly find
out how far they can go.'

T. S. Eliot

When I first met Freyja in 2015, she came across as softly
spoken but quietly at ease among a group of strangers – one
of those people who seemed to have their life sorted. Yet, it
turned out, for a long time she had felt lost, without a sense
of direction. At work she had held herself back, too afraid of
failing. She'd avoided opportunities to present her ideas to
her colleagues, encouraging others in her team to do so
instead. She'd been 'mortified' by the thought of speaking
and maybe failing publicly, so she'd simply not allowed
herself to do so. However, this had changed after she took up
climbing. Now she was leading workshops at work, standing
up in front of her colleagues and strangers, doing more and
more outside of her comfort zone. She'd learnt that 'the
more I do a climbing route that scares me, the more familiar

it gets. The more I do workshop facilitation, the easier it becomes. I wasn't pushing myself as much as I wanted to because I was avoiding failure. Now I give myself a pep talk on the wall and in these professional situations too. I think to myself, I've got this. What's the worst that could happen.'

In 2015 Freyja moved town for a new job and didn't know anyone in the area. Isolated, she decided to seek help. A life coach had suggested she find some activities that made her 'soul sing', so she joined Explorers Connect. Two years later, in 2017, Freyja told me how much that decision had meant to her and how she'd found a new passion for climbing and for life. Her first adventure with me in 2015 had been to climb Snowdon (Wales's highest mountain) on the easiest route, the Pyg Track, which involves an uphill hike but no climbing or exposure ('exposure' means a high risk of injury or death in the event of a false step – imagine standing on top of the Empire State Building looking down on New York with the barricades removed). Freya was an experienced hiker and was geared up for a fun but familiar day in the mountains. But the day before the climb, the guide and the other members of her team brought up the option that it would be perfect weather to try a more challenging route, the Snowdon Horseshoe, which includes the famous and very much exposed knife's edge ridge of Crib Goch, with 400 feet drops on either side. Freyja was terrified, yet frustrated her fear was getting in the way of what she wanted to do. Given the choice between joining the group on the Pyg Track or joining her friends on the greater challenge, she decided to go for it.

With just enough room to put one foot in front of the other, Freya and the team scrambled in single file along the very narrow ridge of rock that separated the two valleys below. While the views across Snowdonia mountain range were spectacular, so were the drops. 'I was scared but I just kept looking forward and, as a group, we managed the whole Horseshoe,' she told me. 'I'm still scared of it, but I'd made a step.' Freyja had pushed herself well outside of her comfort zone. She'd taken that first step to stretch herself. A few weeks later, Freyja had gone to an indoor climbing centre for the first time. By the end of the day, she was thoroughly enjoying it and had decided to go climbing every week. At first, each time Freyja attended she felt incredibly anxious, but she has since realised how significant this was in relation to her pushing through. 'That fearful feeling would normally have stopped me,' Freyja said. 'The anxiety would usually lead to my thinking I was not good enough and that would make me give up. But I kept going every week because I knew, once I was on the wall and climbing, all that anxiety would disappear.' Freyja learnt through experience that the anticipation was worse than the event. And that's even despite the fact that she fell off once: 'The worst thing that *could* happen, *had* happened, but the world hadn't stopped turning. I stopped feeling scared and started to really enjoy it. I've spent most of my life as a perfectionist, beating myself up and seeing myself as a failure for not knowing something. Now, instead, I started to allow myself to question my limitations and be more curious.'

Freyja had joined Malvern Mountaineering Club and had never looked back. Several years later, Freya still climbs at least once a week as lead climber. But it's not just her head for heights that has changed. An introvert who had always spent most of her time in her head, Freyja has discovered her newfound boldness extends into other areas of her life. She has become more confident in social situations and at work. In her career she was always looking for someone to give her permission, but after climbing she learnt to set her own agendas. She knows that confidence came from climbing: 'It's about knowing that if I fail, the worst that could happen is that I'll fall off the wall, dangle uncomfortably for a bit, but that's it – the world won't end. Now I'm taking that mindset back into work.' When Freyja's on the wall, she's pushing herself, reaching out for handholds, and now she's doing the same in life too. Reaching out, risking a fall, but knowing she can handle it. This has increased her ability to reach for targets she'd never attempted before.

By noticing what she'd learnt through climbing and applying it to her everyday life, Freyja removed her limitations, and her life began to change: 'Climbing is now a metaphor for my life. It has given me confidence enough to push my personal boundaries.' Freyja purposefully applies climbing situations, even language, to her work and life, allowing her to measure risk and reward in a new, emboldened way. For example, Freyja climbs using two different techniques, with a top-rope, which feels much more secure, or lead-climbing, which is more advanced and feels riskier. When she climbs using a top-rope, she can attempt much more challenging routes up a wall than when she is using the more exposed-feeling lead-climbing technique. This is not because she can't physically climb the tougher routes; it's her head that is holding her back: 'The top-rope lets me be bold. So now, when I face challenges in life and at work, I ask myself, What's my top-rope? What helps me be bold?'

The pressure to perform well and meet goals at work made Freyja anxious and her fear of failing stopped her from stretching herself to meet those goals. Prior to starting her climbing hobby, Freyja loved learning and was open to experience but admits she wasn't open to risking failure in case it made her look bad. Freyja saw failure as a negative thing and would avoid it. Avoiding failure stopped her from pushing herself, which meant she was stuck in the same place. Climbing has taught her that she has to risk falling and failing: 'If you stay in a fixed shape on the wall, your muscles will eventually fail, and you are guaranteed to fall. So, you need to keep changing shape to move. That's what I was doing in life; I was staying in the same shape. And that wasn't working for me.' Freyja had to try a different way in life, just like she did on the wall. Doing so has reshaped her life. 'The vertical wall is a puzzle to solve,' Freyja explained. 'You have to try one way, and if that doesn't work, you have to try something else, but you have to keep trying, keep experimenting. The kit will hold.' Freyja recognised that staying put was limiting her. Experimenting with different ways of thinking, doing things that stretched her and risking failing has emboldened her no end.

Freyja is a lot more confident, a lot less anxious in social situations and is more willing to step out of her comfort zone now. She's leading workshops, standing up in front of her colleagues and total strangers, something that BC (before climbing) would have left her frozen with fear. In 2017, two years after she started climbing, Freyja arranged to spend the night on a portaledge (a platform a bit like a hammock hung from a cliff face) with Explorers Connect. 'I wasn't scared or anxious at all,' Freyja said, smiling with confidence. 'Two years ago, I wouldn't have even contemplated it.' Such is the growth and power of stepping and stretching outside of your comfort zone. 'It's hard to believe how short a time it has taken to make such a great shift in my confidence and approach to life. It makes me smile all the time when I think about it,' Freyja said, beaming. Freya is reaching out in life, stretching herself, and, as a result, she's growing.

The comfort zone

'In the middle of difficulty, lies opportunity.'

Albert Einstein

Most of us live the majority of our time within an invisible circle, our comfort zone, inside of which are the familiar things that make up our life: the people we know, our jobs, our homes and hobbies. We pick up habits and routines and settle into a way of life that is manageable and comfortable. The comfort zone is important, because it's where we retreat, rest and relax. However, it is also where we can get complacent, disengaged or bored, because we're not developing or experiencing anything new. Just like home, your comfort zone is a place you should frequent, but not somewhere you should reside entirely.

Every time we do something differently or try something novel, we are stepping outside of that invisible circle into the unknown and uncertain – into the stretch zone. It's a challenging and uncomfortable place where we do things we've never done before, where we learn and take risks, and where we're more likely to fail. But it's in the stretch zone that the magic happens; this is where you experience new sensations and learn new things that enable you to grow and, in some cases, transform. This is where you expand your capabilities and can discover a whole range of other gifts: from greater self-esteem, self-actualisation and self-belief to a joyful transcendent feeling of being fully alive.

Once we've taken that step, stretched outside of the familiar, we will notice that the invisible circle that surrounds us, our comfort zone, has grown larger; it's stretched with us, and our life is broader and richer as a result. Consequently, we become more skilled and confident, comfortable in more situations and with more tasks. Our comfort zone expands with experience, along with our abilities. Freyja found that the more she did a climbing route that scared her, the more familiar it got and the better she became. Getting better at things you never thought yourself capable of is a prime reward of stretching outside of your comfort zone.

We find that stretching our comfort zone is enriching, so we keep challenging ourselves, each time learning and growing. Our capacity to want to try new things grows. We become more open to trying and to adventuring. So, we not only improve at whatever activity we've faced, we grow braver too.

Freyja's story demonstrates the core benefits of stretching outside of your comfort zone:

- The feel-good factor that comes from achievement
- Getting better at things
- Growing in confidence
- Becoming more open to trying new things
- Positive transformation across other areas of life

But there is a balance to be struck. Karl Rohnke devised the 'Comfort, Stretch and Panic Zone' model to better understand and communicate the relationship between arousal and performance. This model has an additional area in which we can find ourselves: the panic zone, which is entered when we go past being 'stretched' and find that something is too challenging, daunting or conflicting to the point that it is overwhelming and causes us distress. Rohnke's model is based on the Yerkes–Dodson Law, originally developed by the psychologists Robert Yerkes and John Dodson in 1908. According to their law, peak performance is achieved when people experience a moderate level of pressure. With too much or too little arousal, performance decreases. This ties in with what I've seen on adventures. If Freyja had pushed too hard too soon, she might have frightened herself away from climbing and heights for ever. Some form of challenge is needed in order to optimally function, but when we experience too much or too little pressure, our performance – and our wellbeing – declines.

The same is true when we consider the two hemispheres of the brain and how they are balanced between the right side, which deals with novelty and uncertainty, and the left side, which deals with routine. When we first try something new, the right hemisphere of the brain leads the way, with the left hemisphere taking over once that activity becomes more routine. To be truly engaged and function optimally requires us to mediate between the two. Our brains are wired to respond well to balance: to enjoy the order and security of the comfort zone and a moderate amount of stretching ourselves via new adventures so that we might grow. When we get this balance right, it speaks to the deepest primal part of our neurological and evolutionary self, and it feels instinctively correct. Getting the balance right between novel and routine, between comfort and discomfort, between known and unknown, helps us to function optimally. Modern life leans too much towards comfort, but adventure rectifies this by offering challenge, adversity and uncertainty within the stretch zone. And it is only by regularly moving between the comfort and stretch zones that we are able to grow.

The growth mindset

'One can choose to go back toward safety or forward toward growth. Growth must be chosen again and again; fear must be overcome again and again.'

Abraham Maslow, psychologist

Freyja's experience of climbing moved her from believing you're either good at something or terrible at it to knowing that practice and effort helps you become better at things. Understanding this concept of growth is important, because simply believing that we get better with practice has the power to make us behave differently. This has been evidenced by the Stanford University psychologist Carol Dweck through thirty years of research into our beliefs around learning and talent, which led her to coin the terms 'growth mindset' and 'fixed mindset'. The more of a growth mindset we have, the more we are willing to risk failure, because we know that, with practice, we improve our abilities. It's worth the risk, because trying is the only way we'll progress, and a failure will just alert us to what we need to work on. A fixed mindset, on the other hand, limits us. We don't try, because we see no point – we are either bright or not, talented or not, can present workshops or not – and if we think that our ability is innate, a failure can be unsettling, because it makes us doubt how good we are. The fear of failure keeps us stuck in the comfort zone, unable to grow.

People with a fixed mindset are cautious to avoid mistakes, and they may get defensive when someone suggests they made a mistake, because they measure themselves by their failures. People with a growth mindset instead show resilience and perseverance when they've made mistakes; they become more motivated to work harder. So, you can imagine how much having a growth or fixed mindset can affect our lives. Freyja was able to move from a fixed to a growth mindset based on the evidence she was experiencing for herself as she pushed herself further than she thought was possible. The more she climbed, the more she believed in her own capabilities. Once you've taken that first step, the possibilities grow with you. That's what happened to Freyja, and that's what happened to me when I took my own first step outside of my comfort zone.

My first big adventure

I've often been called fearless, given the number of expeditions I've been on, yet I've spent a lot of my life petrified about not doing well enough. In fact, my time at school was plagued by feeling I was not good enough and a fear of failing. Fear of the future made me work hard and follow the rules. I toed the line and did as I was told, as I didn't have the confidence to question or to stand up to the status quo. The story I told myself was that if I didn't get the right grades, I wouldn't get into the right university, and I'd end up in a dead-end job and be a failure. The rest of my life would essentially be ruined if I didn't get each step absolutely right. Hallmarks of a fixed mindset.

Not only was this story inaccurate (some of my most successful friends from school were definitely not top of the class), it was also paralysing and limiting. The pressure was immense, and rather than motivating me and spurring me on, the fear of not getting good enough grades gnawed away at me. I even felt like I'd failed when I got a B in an exam I took a year early.

My school had predicted my grades wouldn't be good enough for me to get into the top universities, so I hadn't applied. But I actually did better than anyone had expected, partly due to the fact I'd rediscovered adventure through the Duke of Edinburgh's Award scheme I mentioned in chapter two. My newfound confidence, born in adventure, helped me reframe my fear of failure in a more productive way, and I emerged with straight As in my A levels, enough to potentially get me in to Oxford University the following year.

This gave me a window, a gap in which to do something else. With a year of no structured, regulated learning ahead of me, I had the freedom to make a decision for the first time in my life about what I wanted to do. Not what other people expected me to do, but what my heart called me towards. My micro-expeditions in the British countryside had given me the confidence to act. Gap years in the 1990s weren't as popular as they are today. My parents wanted me to get work experience and save money for university during the year off, but the whispers of adventure grew louder.

I'd first heard those whispers sitting with my grandfather Niels in my grandparents' countryside cottage, surrounded by his books and African artefacts. He would quietly tell me stories of his time in Africa as a zoology professor, where he taught at universities in Uganda, Nigeria and Lesotho, while I would gently flick through his albums of small, square, faded black-and-white photographs, mesmerised by the menagerie of monkeys and elephants looking back at me. As he softly recounted tales of the time he walked across a desert with a tribal elder, of the escaped rescue elephant and how he was one of the first to study the behaviour of mountain gorillas while he lived in the forests, the seed for my love of Africa was sown, further nurtured by the spears, wicker Basotho hat and drums dotted around the cottage. These sparks fuelled a curiosity to see Africa for myself.

Until now, my fear of failure had stopped me from venturing off the path that had been chosen for me towards the path that piqued my curiosity. So, I did the first non-compliant thing I had ever done in my life. Against my parents' wishes, I decided to go to Africa.

Those childhood stories from my grandfather inspired me just enough to overcome my fear and act on my newly formed confidence. So, I stepped outside of my compliant comfort zone, found a biological fieldwork expedition to Tanzania that I could join and booked a flight. Apart from a European exchange trip and family holidays, I'd never left the country. But here I was, fresh out of school, about to embark on a year-long adventure, studying monkeys in the wilds of the African jungle and travelling in this curious continent. Just the act of deciding to go was empowering; I was already benefitting from the adventure. And besides, some biological fieldwork would be 'good for the CV'. I didn't realise then quite how profound that explorer instinct was and how much I would have missed out on had I not taken that first step outside of my comfort zone.

That first step was the hardest and, as such, the most important of all the steps I've ever taken. Because it was *my* step, my very own step into the unknown, a place where I was totally responsible for myself and my decisions. Terrified but determined (I'd told my friends I was going, so no backing out now), I flew to Dar es Salaam.

For the next three months, I worked in the remote monsoonal forests of the Uluguru Mountains as part of a biological expedition to measure the biodiversity of plants and animals in the area. As a budding biologist off to study zoology at Oxford the following year, I was eager to learn and got stuck in. The team was led by a passionate if a little erratic biologist. Spitting cobras and other snakes found their way into our not particularly organised camp, and we ended up inadvertently swimming with crocodiles (which still makes me shudder to think about).

A few weeks into the expedition, I was given my own study to collect data for. It involved going into the forest on my own each day to monitor the closest troupe of wild black-and-white colobus monkeys so I could record what they were eating. I thankfully discovered a troupe thirty minutes' walk from camp, so each day I would follow them as they spread across their territory.

We weren't given much training, but we were taught to stomp our feet when moving about the forest. I learnt that most jungle critters will get out of your way when you walk heavy-footed through the jungle – especially snakes. Except the lazier puff adder, which will happily sit and wait for you. A lot of my time patrolling the jungle was spent looking down instead of enjoying the view, because I did not want to accidentally step on a puff adder, especially if I was on my own – which I often was. Some might question the expedition leader's decision to send me, an inexperienced eighteen-year-old British girl from Bristol with minimal training, deep into the jungle on my own every day. And goodness knows what my parents would've thought. But I survived, and it was actually the making of me. There were almost no rules, and I was given a freedom I'd never known before, which was terrifying yet thrilling.

I learnt to carry the correct essentials and emergency kit, to dress appropriately in long sleeves and trousers, tucking my trousers into my socks to protect against bugs crawling upwards. I learnt this particular lesson the hard way when I inadvertently stood on a trail of siafu ants, which swarmed up my legs, coordinating a synchronised biting attack once they had reached my shoulder. Slapping myself all over, I had to resort to jumping in the river to try to convince them to let go. I was learning I could make mistakes and still survive; even better, I could learn and progress because of them.

To monitor what the monkeys were eating, I learnt all I could about the trees in that area. The troupe lived high in the canopy, but I could spy on them with binoculars to determine whether they were eating fresh shoots, berries or leaves. They would also drop half-eaten meals, offering me another opportunity to examine which parts of which species they were eating. At first, they'd also drop less pleasant missiles to discourage me from following them: their favourite evasive technique was to poo on me.

Every day, as I stood watching these wild monkeys in awe, I'd have to pinch myself that I was really here managing a biological study of my very own. Just a couple of months earlier I'd been in a school uniform. I'd toed the line and complied. Now, here I was walking freely through the African jungle on my own, with only my colobus-monkey troupe for company. I felt more alive and more part of the world than I had ever felt before.

And then something magical happened. After a month of following my pooping, leaping black-and-white friends, I noticed I was being allowed to get closer. One day, I was sitting so high up a steep bank that I was level with some of the lower branches in which the colobus were sitting. I was no longer craning my neck to see them but looking out across the lower canopy at the same level, communing with them. Not quite close enough to touch, but I could see their individual faces and expressions, just as they could see mine. They had stopped aiming poo missiles at me as they'd become accustomed to my presence. It seemed they no longer saw me as a threat and had accepted me as an honorary member of their troupe, an uninvited but benevolent visitor who was welcome for a while as long as I didn't get in the way.

My status was confirmed when there was a commotion below. My research team appeared on the valley floor, putting out bat traps. Clearly agitated, the alarm was raised – familiar cautionary chattering calls, sudden bounding and retreating – as the colobus rallied against the intruders. A few missiles and a little poo-rain and they were gone. Rather than feeling annoyed that my team had disturbed my opportunity for observation, instead my heart swelled with pride. They were *my* colobus. They no longer ran or threw missiles at me like they had done with these strangers. While they were unwelcome and avoided, I was now welcomed and accepted. A huge beaming smile spread across my face as I silently sat enjoying the moment. Little old me! I was doing something special.

The days I had put in chasing through the trees, worrying about snakes and getting lost, concerned I might never be able to study the monkeys properly, had enabled me to travel in and out of another world. No matter what else happened on this adventure in Africa, I had these magical moments that would last for ever. Where before I had never felt so scared, now I had never felt so alive. And if I could do this, what else might be possible? I suddenly felt incredibly capable, and the world seemed so full of possibilities. It was in that moment that I learnt how putting yourself out there, outside of your comfort zone, is how you get to experience magic. There's no short cut. Magic comes to those who answer the call to adventure.

Since that magical moment with my monkeys in the wilds of Tanzania, there have been many more: watching sunrise from the summit of an Indonesian volcano, swimming with whale sharks in Mozambique and the moment I jumped out of a helicopter into the solitude of the Mosquito Coast jungle. I would have missed *all* of those magic moments and more had I not pushed myself outside of my comfort zone that very first time, had I not faced my fears and, crucially, had I not risked failing.

And it's a good job my first adventure removed my fear of

failure, because there have been plenty of failures to learn from during my adventures over the years. Including the first expedition that I led myself, which involved our team looking for Bactrian camels in China for six weeks and finding none. Or getting lost in the Amazon for twenty-four hours before finding the river again and the route home. Or nearly getting run over by a Russian tanker off the coast of Scotland while in a twenty-four-feet rowing boat. Those failures and many others have taught me specific lessons, but, most of all, they have also taught me that it is impossible to live without failing at something, unless you live so cautiously that you might as well not have lived at all – in which case, you have failed by default.

Consequently, I refuse to live a life limited by a fear of failure. On the contrary, I've done things because there was a high likelihood of failure and I wanted to stretch myself and learn as much as I possibly could by giving it a try. Like the time I formed the first female crew (and second-ever boat) to row nonstop around Britain unaided, attempting a world record, despite having rarely been at sea for more than a day trip and being a terrible rower.

Rowing into the stretch zone

After fifteen years of leading expeditions and making wildlife and adventure films in remote jungles and deserts, I'd grown accustomed and felt comfortable in those habitats and felt that I wasn't really stretching myself any more. So, to challenge myself, I decided to row around Britain, despite never having done any rowing in the ocean before. I chose to do this because I didn't know if I would be able to do it and *because* so many people had failed trying. It was precisely because we were not guaranteed success that I wanted to do it. It wasn't the ocean rowing I specifically wanted to test myself against – there were some great opportunities to join races across the Atlantic Ocean, for example. But that path was comparatively well-trodden, and the failure rate is relatively low and mostly due to bad luck. For me, it was the unknown of the row around the UK that called me to try. Dozens of crews had attempted it and at that time only one had succeeded. (Even ten years later, only six boats had managed the row, and of that small fraternity, there was still only one female crew to have made it round.) No one could tell us how to do it; we'd have to figure it out ourselves. What a challenge!

Even Sir Ranulph Fiennes, known as the world's greatest living explorer and famous for sawing off his own fingers due to frostbite, said it would be 'arduous'. And it was the most arduous and uncomfortable adventure I'd ever undertaken. We completed the row in a twenty-four-feet by five-feet rowing boat with no sail and no engine in fifty-two days, rowing for twelve hours each day for nearly two months.

The worst moments were the painful stress-fractured fingers, muscle wastage, memory loss and delusions that came from rowing for two hours, sleeping for two hours and repeating it all for more than seven weeks across 2,100 miles. We were very nearly killed on a couple of occasions. I would not set sail on this challenge now I am the mother of a young child, but at that time we were four adults who understood the risks. The UK is home to some of the strongest conflicting currents and the busiest shipping lanes in the world, so navigating those waters was testing to say the least.

But, amid the suffering, there were many magical moments, and, no matter how bad things got, I would not have missed those experiences for the world: from the pair of orca swimming up to the boat in Scotland and the countless seals playing hide and seek with us to the puffins, basking sharks and, most memorably, the indescribable feeling when a superpod of hundreds of dolphins escorted us through Milford Haven shipping lanes as we strived to avoid the juggernaut tankers.

There was the joy we found in the little things too: rowing into the sunrise, singing along to tunes from the precious radio and the pure joy of finding a bag of nuts in your weekly ration pack. And the moment when, south of Portland Bill, the sea was as smooth as a mirror, with the horizon no longer visible. It felt like we were inside a blue-and-white glass marble. We all stopped rowing and stayed still in that moment, awestruck by the incredible beauty of it.

You don't get to feel that alive unless you leave your comfort zone. If I'd stayed at home, none of this magic would have been mine. Neither would I have done any of it had I continued to be so fearful of failure, so afraid to look foolish. I've learnt through adventure that the reason for existing is not to fill your life with days but to fill your days with life. So many of us are afraid of failing, whereas actually what we should really be afraid of is *not trying*. Life takes on a new dimension when you decide to try the things you want to and not just the things that you know you can already do. To truly dare to fail, to do something beyond myself and completely outside of my comfort zone, was my motivating force, because I knew that finding novel challenges is how we grow and how we find out what we are capable of. As it turns out, despite being open to failing, we didn't fail in our aim to row round Britain unaided. We succeeded.

Get comfortable being uncomfortable

Life has become too comfortable. Our evolutionary bias to seek comfort wasn't designed for the twenty-first century. We need to turn that craving for comfort on its head. To regain balance, we need to voluntarily seek out discomfort. As we learnt from the research, experiencing a moderate level of pressure puts our minds and bodies into a position of peak performance, allowing us to achieve and get better at things. In turn, this makes us more confident and braver. All of this helps us to grow, but it also feels good. The times when I have felt I am the best version of myself were invariably moments on adventures.

I have always had the conviction that I will never stop exploring, never stop adventuring (when I'm seventy years old, I have plans to swim the English Channel), and by analysing the benefits of stretching ourselves, I can understand why I feel like this. Because to keep striving is to keep living, to keep risking failure to find out what I'm capable of, to experience magic and discover my best self, that is worth feeling a little uncomfortable for.

And it seems I'm not the only one. The huge rise in popularity of challenging, uncomfortable pursuits, such as Tough Mudder, which not only drags you through the mud and drops you in icy waterholes but also shocks you with 10,000 volts of electricity as part of a 'fun' day out, demonstrates that others are seeking out something to put them through their paces too. Adventure does that. When life gets too comfort-able, what our mind and body craves is adventure. If we face our fears and build bravery, if we lean in to our weaknesses in order to develop our strengths, and if we dare to fail in order to learn, we can open up a whole new world of possi-bilities and adventures.

Eight

To Strengthen Relationships

'Shared joy is a double joy; shared sorrow is half a sorrow.'
Swedish proverb

Decades of research reveals that supportive relationships are vital for both our physical and psychological wellbeing, supporting our mental health, aiding recovery from illness and even positively impacting our longevity. The longest study of adult life that's ever been carried out, the Harvard Study of Adult Development, has since 1938 studied the lives of 724 men over a period of eighty-two years to discover what makes them happy and healthy. The findings show that good relationships are what keep us happier and healthier: social connections are good for us and loneliness is not. But it's not the quantity of friends that matters; it's the quality of those friendships.

Warm and supportive relationships are protective, whereas high-conflict, low-trust relationships are damaging. Bickering between couples, siblings or groups was seen by the study as having minimal impact on individuals' longevity, as long as the people in the relationship felt they could count on each other's support during tough times – that sense of trust was important. In this way, supportive relationships literally act as a buffer to the stresses and strains of modern life.

We can strengthen the relationships we have with those we adventure with, and we can take the trust, improved communication and compassion learnt on adventures to nourish our existing relationships at home too. Just like Amina did.

Amina Smith-Gul struggled with substance abuse, anger and suicidal episodes as a consequence of trauma she had experienced as a teenager. In 2016, at the age of seventeen, she became homeless. Four years later, she was the opening speaker at my conference Adventure Mind in London. Now a respected youth leader, she stood in front of hundreds of people and shared her story of transformation through adventure. Born in Deptford, southeast London, Amina's three siblings were much older than her, and her parents split up while she was a child. Amina's terminally ill nan moved into her family home when she was eleven, and Amina and her mum took on the role of carer between them. This was tough, but when her grandmother died in 2011, life got even tougher. Over the years that followed, she lost several people close to her through violence: Amina's aunt was murdered by a relative in an honour killing in 2012, and her close friend was stabbed to death two years after that.

'Because of these traumatic events, I struggled a lot with anger,' explained Amina, who then found herself homeless after losing her temper at home. Amina was smoking cannabis at the time, and her parents thought she was exhibiting paranoid and psychotic tendencies. When Amina went to the doctor, rather than giving the diagnosis her parents had been expecting, the doctor suggested her symptoms were to do with misunderstood and unresolved anger. So, Amina was referred for counselling to deal with 'a secondary emotion that comes from hurt'.

Late in 2016, keen to overcome her issues and get a roof over her head, Amina took part in Lewisham borough's youth-pathway programme, which helps vulnerable young people to find a home. But it wasn't easy. Amina found the hostel system challenging, being with twenty girls she didn't know, with minimal space or privacy.

Early in 2018, Amina was thrown a lifeline. A representative from the British Exploring Society (BES), which runs expeditions for sixteen- to twenty-five-year-olds, invited Amina to join a training weekend in the UK. Despite feeling out of place, Amina went ahead with it. That small brave step was the beginning of a life-changing experience that would take Amina from being an angry homeless teenager to a well-respected mentor in her local community. Later that year, now nineteen, Amina was invited to go on a three-week BES expedition into the Peruvian Amazon. Coincidentally, the very first BES Amazon expedition was the one I'd established sixteen years earlier with Alice. When I heard Amina's story, I was delighted to discover it was (and still is) running and working for young people. Although scared of what might await her in the jungle, Amina didn't want to let the group leaders down. And having read biographies about people stepping out of their comfort zone and achieving success, she agreed to go.

Once in the jungle, without modern amenities or phones to pull attention away from the people around her, Amina noticed cliques and clusters dissolved in favour of 'real life' – the kind of life that happens where people and nature meet each other, with little else in between. 'You can be isolated at home,' Amina said. 'People rarely come together to do anything. I began to see the world in a different way.' The back-to-basics lifestyle also gave the young explorers the chance to be more present, to notice and savour their surroundings and to create lasting memories. 'Having no phones gave us the chance to play card games and sing songs together,' Amina said. 'I've never really done that with my mates in London.' Instead of looking down at phones, everyone looked up and engaged with each other.

At first, Amina and the other young people on the expedition were cautious of each other. But they soon realised they needed to work together. Before long, they were eating, sleeping, laughing and thriving together. 'We'd watch the sunrise every day, and hear the same bird make a sound like a donkey,' Amina said, smiling. 'We called it the donkey bird; we didn't know its real name. But we did learn a lot that we hadn't known before, including where our food waste was and what was eating it, because we had to leave no trace. This was real.' In the jungle, actions have consequences; what people do matters.

As a result, Amina noticed a simple truth of adventuring: when you sit round a campfire or journey through a jungle together, you have deeper, more meaningful conversations than you have at the pub or in the office. There is something about staring into the flickering embers that invokes a primeval ancestral memory. Campfire communication is more intimate, which leads to a deeper connection, along with greater affinity, empathy and authenticity. You become yourself, and you see others becoming themselves, too. Adventures generate authenticity, maybe because many of the trappings of modern life that we hide behind are stripped away as you 'cross the threshold' into the great unknown or the great outdoors. This in turn leads to the strengthening of relationships. You can work with people for years in an office and never know them at all. Shuffling around the coffee machine or the printer, the same old questions arise; the same polite chat goes to and fro. Indeed, you might be considered a bit weird if you delved deeper and asked them about their dreams and passions, their deepest worries and fears. But there's something magical that happens when you put that same team in a wood around a campfire, in the rainforest or halfway up a mountain. There's a shared vulnerability and a shared excitement that not only bonds us but rips down those limiting formalities so we can really talk. And in a world where we're so frequently stretched too thin, more depth is a real gift.

I remember putting this idea to the test myself when I spent the night camping on a hillside overlooking Bristol to watch a meteor shower with a group of friends from Explorers Connect. Not only did I see my own city with fresh eyes, I saw my friends with fresh eyes too. We chatted late into the night. No one had phone reception (carefully planned by me), so everyone was present. Instead of the usual perpetual distractions of technology, the rush was replaced by a calm, easy and natural intimacy – that sort of friendliness you only experience on the trail, crammed into a mountain hut or huddled around an open fire. We talked about our beliefs and worries, our plans and passions – a totally different set of conversations to those we'd have had if we'd all met in a pub instead.

As such, you need not always travel to the furthest flung corners of the globe to deepen and strengthen relationships. A simple night hike on a mountain or a camp around an open fire can be transformative enough. Even without the adversities of a grand expedition, just an evening of adventure camping on a city hill can start the ball rolling.

Perhaps this is why family adventure holidays are becoming more popular, as they can, according to researcher Dr Gill Pomfret from Sheffield Hallam University, 'lead to improved family functioning and, like outdoor therapy, result in improved family communication, trust, collective efficacy, healthy lifestyle and cohesion'. Evening adventures on city hilltops and family adventure holidays are a small way of leaving your normal life behind to do something extraordinary in an unknown place, which builds more meaningful conversations and connections.

At work or school, you can avoid any real interaction with others if you like. In the modern world, we can so easily withdraw from a situation, ignore it and hope it goes away. But there's usually no getting away from fractious issues when you're in the middle of nowhere, depending on each other for safety. Occasionally, adventure teams fail under this pressure and break up. However, in my experience, living cheek to jowl every day in a team usually means you must work together; there's no escaping connection, so you have to find ways to communicate and get on. Doing so has led me to develop some of my strongest friendships, while also helping me to appreciate views that are different to mine and developing my empathy. This social development happens more readily on adventures, because you're all in the same challenging situation. In this way, adventure acts as a tremendous equaliser, encouraging cross-cultural tolerance and understanding.

Relationships are often about having a shared responsibility for one another, and this is amplified in outdoor challenges. None of Amina's team knew each other, having been put together after the training weekend, but they quickly became very close. Knowing they were together in a remote part of the rainforest, far from help, where anything could happen, fostered a deep sense of camaraderie. 'If people were feeling homesick, together we helped them,' Amina said. 'Nobody was alone. We had to check each other for diarrhoea and vomiting and look out for each other constantly.' On one occasion, while trekking through the jungle, one of Amina's group fell into the water. Soaked through and aware of the long journey ahead of her, she began to cry: 'We all stopped to reassure her, have a group hug and talk through her feelings. We managed it as a group with care and togetherness.'

When you're responsible for other people on an expedition, you also tend to develop your communication skills and become better at listening, because you need to be able to understand and respond well to others' needs. The positive impact of this can be huge. The greater sense of kinship and empathy with other humans strengthens relationships – not only with those you're sharing the adventure with, but also with those you return home to.

Experiencing challenging times together meant Amina's group got to know each other better and quicker. They relied on each other, building trust and friendships that would last, as Amanda Challans also found after she overcame her ME and completed her world-record-breaking row: 'Those bonds between teammates are irreplaceable. There's no one else in the world apart from those who have shared in this journey with you, who know what you've been through. That's where lifelong friendships are created. I still keep in touch with people I went on adventures with seventeen years ago. I could call them up at any moment, and it would seem like yesterday! These unique groups of people I've adventured with have become the people I truly trust and have a huge amount of respect for.'

The same is true for me. Indeed, most of my longest-lasting and strongest friendships are with ex-adventure teammates. Spending months cutting through jungles, working in deserts and dealing with crises together far from home creates a bond like no other. That includes Jim, my partner of twenty years: we met on expedition in Lesotho. And my friend Nick, who as I write this, is outside my office window helping us to plant trees in an effort to rewild our fields: we went on several expeditions together, including to southern Africa, Sinai, the Amazon and Alaska, between 1998 and 2003. These true friendships were made over a relatively short period of time, but, years later, we can rekindle that magic we shared in the wild. There exists a lasting bond between teammates, even if you've only known each other for a few weeks, because of what you've endured side by side.

There are several reasons why I think adventure is so effective at strengthening relationships. First, adventuring provides concentrated, undistracted time in each other's company. According to research from the University of Kansas published in the *Journal of Social and Personal Relationships* in 2018, it usually takes between forty to sixty hours to form a casual friendship, eighty to 100 hours to become a friend and about 200 hours to become good friends or best friends. Overnight or multiday adventure fast-tracks this process, because you wake, eat, work, rest and sleep in each other's company. You also do so away from the distractions of everyday life that can dilute time spent together, like watching TV, keeping up to date with social media streams and phone notifications.

The second reason adventure is so good for our friendships is because it provides an experience through which we survive and overcome adversity together. Research published in 2014 in the *Journal of the Association for Psychological Science* found that shared pain or adversity brings people together, acting like a kind of 'social glue' that fosters bonding and solidarity between members of a group. Following experiments conducted by University of Queensland researchers, students who performed painful tasks (from submerging hands in painfully cold water to performing squats) showed a greater degree of group bonding than those who performed pain-free versions of the tasks. What's more, in addition to a sense of solidarity between members of the group who'd endured the same challenging experience, individuals were found to cooperate more readily with each other in future tasks too. Further research published by Bernadette von Dawans in Germany in 2012 and 2018 found that acute stress leads to greater cooperative, social and friendly behaviour via a 'tend-and-befriend' pattern amongst men and women. Stronger relationships are forged in the crucible of adventure when people rise to challenges and overcome obstacles together. Like metal that's heated and hammered, those bonds become solid and resilient, immune to the knocks to come.

In my own experience, like Amina, sharing adversities begets better bonds. Indeed, some of my favourite adventures have been the ones that have gone wrong. Take the time a group of us planned to go on a weekend walk across Dartmoor in 2013. With high winds and rain forecast for the next forty-eight hours, half the group cancelled. It was just down to the final five: me, my partner Jim, Liz, Caroline and Shawn. We met in a wet car park on the southern edge of the moor, and although none of us said anything, I think we were all wondering why we hadn't bailed, too.

With rain pouring down nonstop like buckets of water and gusts of wind taking our breath away, it should have been dismal, but it turned out to be one of my favourite and most memorable UK adventures. This was partly due to the banter between Jim and me – he had sworn never to camp in bad weather again, having previously spent six weeks on an ice cap with a leaky tent and damp sleeping bag. Yet here we were. But the main reason I enjoyed it so much was the camaraderie fostered as the rain poured down. The dismal weather and relentless damp became a prime source of giggles for everyone, as were the slugs in Jim's coffee mug and his wet tobacco. I have fond memories of my four adventure teammates because of their humour and tolerance, and seven years later there is only one whom I have lost contact with, despite the rest of us living in different areas and our lives having no other connection but a few adventures. I know we could all meet up now and laugh about it again, as if it happened yesterday. It was all the more adventurous for the adversity. For those who cancelled, it might all have been too much, but for those left standing, it gave us a chance to live adventurously as we braved the bad weather together.

And we were rewarded sufficiently for our perseverance. For most of the morning, we were wrapped in a foggy blanket covering everything around us, so you couldn't even see the grass further than a dozen metres in any direction. Then, all of a sudden, a gust of wind blew a hole in the clag, tearing a window onto the world. Now, instead of walking into a grey unknown, we were walking towards a perfectly framed and beautiful picture of moorland landscape – all sweeping hills into the horizon – an image that is indelibly burnt into my memory.

Evidently, shared experience and adversity act as a catalyst for deeper connection. The same is true of vulnerability. Research professor Brené Brown has found that being vulnerable increases trust and our ability to relate to one another. 'There can be no intimacy – emotional intimacy, spiritual intimacy, physical intimacy – without vulnerability,' said Brown, who conducted thousands of interviews and came to the conclusion that the key to connection is vulnerability. 'One of the reasons there is such an intimacy deficit today is because we don't know how to be vulnerable. It's about being honest with how we feel, about our fears, about what we need, and, asking for what we need. Vulnerability is glue that holds intimate relationships together.'

And we are rarely more vulnerable than when we face our fears and push ourselves past our limits during adventurous pursuits. When you're part of a team on an adventure, out of your comfort zone, participating in new activities in unknown places, you are never more reliant on others. And this shared vulnerability breeds trust, because you have no other option. This level of trust is rare in the comfortable, modern world – to truly trust in others to the extent that you are putting your physical and mental wellbeing in their hands, even your life – but it happens all the time in adventure.

Trust is like social glue, essential for camaraderie. That feeling of being able to count on each other binds relationships together. Amina explained to me that while trekking through the jungle her team would routinely warn each other of potential dangers; if someone was tired, they all took a break together, and if anyone got ill, they would look after them. Amina's Amazon team are now spread around the world, but they have an active Snapchat group to stay in touch, wishing each other happy birthday and regularly checking in with each other, like they did in the jungle. 'The trust we built was so important,' Amina said. 'We knew we all had to have each other's backs. We still do.' The sense of trust you develop in other people while on adventure transfers into regular life once you're back home. You recognise that people, on the whole, are decent and are likely to do the right thing and be able to help if needed. That can be a huge realisation for anyone who has been let down by those close to them in the past.

On an adventure, you learn to see the good in people. You also learn to find the good in yourself. It was during the expedition that Amina discovered she had leadership qualities. This lesson was learnt on a trek where the team had been given the challenge of directing the route themselves. 'We got a bit lost,' she said. 'We were all stressed and hungry, and everyone wanted to give up rather than risk going deeper into the jungle.' Amina felt they should keep going and urged her team to carry on. However, after a group discussion, she felt the pressure to go along with her teammates and eventually agreed perhaps they should turn back after all. At this point, the main leader took Amina aside and encouraged her to trust her opinion and use her leadership skills in a positive way to encourage her peers. She did, and the team carried on: 'When we finally arrived at our destination, we got to see pink dolphins in a lake in the jungle!' It was a magical and rewarding experience they simply wouldn't have had if they'd turned back: 'It was even sweeter, even more satisfying to see the dolphins because we nearly didn't make it.' That day, Amina learnt to trust in herself and to keep going despite difficulties, because the satisfaction of persevering is greater than the journey endured: 'It's about not giving up on the way to where I'm trying to get in life.'

These days, Amina's family simply doesn't recognise her as the same person she was before her expedition. Amina herself noticed how much the experience of adventure had changed her. 'I felt different,' she said. 'It instilled in me the importance of serving others.' She'd found her tribe, and she'd also found her purpose.

Since returning from that expedition, Amina has turned her life around. She now works for Wandsworth Community Empowerment Network on a project called Black Minds Matter, a mental-health and wellbeing initiative: 'Their motto is "As we rise, we lift", something I now have a strong belief in.' Having experienced significant challenges herself, Amina now helps other young people, facilitating and leading workshops with them and sharing how the expedition helped her to learn resilience and what's possible in life: 'People in my community don't tend to be comfortable going outdoors, but now I can share my story with them.'

As a result of going on an adventure and her subsequent drive to pass on what she's learnt and experienced to others, Amina has escaped the trap of anger she previously felt locked in and has regained control of her life: 'I am a better person because of adventure. Before I left for the Amazon, there was a lot of chaos in my life. I wasn't organised or clear about what my next steps would be. Life was happening to me, but I felt like I didn't have control. The expedition experience was life-changing. I realised that life is about choices, and that I am in control of my own life and destiny. I'm committed to trying to be the type of person who helps and encourages others.' As such, Amina is putting her new abilities to the best use possible by building strong relationships. In doing so, she's not only boosting her own wellbeing but helping others to do the same.

Nine

To Find Joy

'If you cannot understand that there is something in man which responds to the challenge of this mountain and goes out to meet it, that the struggle is the struggle of life itself upward and forever upward, then you won't see why we go. What we get from this adventure is just sheer joy. And joy is after all the end of life. We do not live to eat and make money. We eat and make money to be able to enjoy life. That is what life means and what life is for.'

George Mallory, mountaineer

It's morning, deep in the East African countryside. Goodu's son Mahiya glances again over his shoulder, grins and beckons me to keep up. His eyes shine pure white against the dusty beige landscape and sparkle with mischief. His confidence is only outshone by his playful misbehaviour. At a guess, he's nine or ten years old and my guide for the morning. I'm hoping he's not in the mood to play a prank, as I have no idea where camp is, and I am 100 per cent reliant on him.

Jogging through the grass to keep up with the Hadza boys, I'm aware how noisy I am, clomping in my size-nine boots, compared to the barefoot silence of the children. We continue mostly single file. Initially offended to have been offered a day with the children when I'd asked to experience the hunt, now I'm grateful, given how much effort it's taking me to keep up with these kids. What chance would I have stood keeping pace with the adult men?

Mahiya is lean and fit, wearing three strings of beads and a worn pair of khaki shorts. He carries a simple wooden bow and a handful of arrows, two fur strips on the bow evidence of his recent kills, the fletching on the arrows made of three black-and-white feathers, and the poison on the arrowheads made of the boiled sap of the desert rose, powerful enough to stop an impala. He's picked up the pace, so I assume he's seen something. He darts ahead, and I struggle to keep up.

Despite me being the adult and him the child, here we've swapped roles. I'm the defenceless child in the wilderness, reliant on his guidance. He's not yet a teenager but already at home on the plains of Africa, a master hunter who, along with the other kids, runs stealthily on, oblivious to my difficulties as we pass through Hadza country, the spiked acacia trees and thorn bushes scratching my limbs and the heat making me feel as dehydrated as the brittle cracked African landscape underfoot. By the time I catch up, Mahiya is pulling an arrow from a small bird. I'd seen him stop and pull his arm back, but I was way too slow to spot the bird or know what was happening. I swig more water, amazed at how these kids don't seem to need to drink much at all.

By now I'd spent almost a decade, probably the same amount of time that Mahiya had been alive, travelling round the world, often solo, and leading extreme expeditions, so I secretly like to think of myself as pretty tough. But here's this nine-year-old knocking me down a peg or two.

The scratch on my arm from one of the many thorn bushes is oozing blood, and I feel light-headed from running in the heat. That and the keen awareness that there are lions, baboons and hyena in the bushes around us adds to the fear and frustration. But it doesn't bother me, because I'm loving every minute. In fact, I can't remember the last time I felt such unbounded, joyous excitement. I feel like I'm a nine-year-old kid again. I'm overcome with exhilaration. Here I am galloping through the bush, hunting with a real tribe. I feel so alive! When did I last do something that took all my concentration and effort and yet with a total lack of inhibition or restraint? The sense of pure freedom washes over me.

Suddenly there's a crashing in the bushes to our left. A large male warthog darts out, head and tusks upright and tail defiantly in the air. When a 100-kilogram hog is charging at you with razor-sharp tusks, it brings to mind the knowledge that these feisty and fast cannonballs regularly fight off leopards, even lions. It's easier to forget, in the moment, that attacks on humans are rare. Fear floods my system but is quickly replaced by relief as he carries on past me. I cast my eyes towards the sun. I've been through a roller coaster of emotions and experiences; so much joy has been found and felt, yet the day has barely begun.

I had spent the previous week with Goodu, an elder of the Hadza tribe near Lake Eyasi in northern Tanzania, to research their traditions and survival techniques for a BBC TV documentary. As well as the inaccessible tribes deep in the Amazon jungle, the Hadza are some of the last remaining hunter-gatherers on the planet, foraging for food rather than growing it via agriculture. There are thought to be around 1,000 to 1,200 Hadza, and half of them still live exclusively as full-time foragers in an existence that has changed very little from 10,000 years ago. Men collect honey and use bows and arrows to hunt mammals and birds, while women dig wild tubers and gather fruit and berries. They grow no food, raise no livestock. Camps of thirty or so move every few weeks in response to the availability of food and resources. A magnet for researchers for more than seven decades, the Hadza's nomadic way of life may be the closest analogue we have to the way our African ancestors lived.

The Hadza also have no calendars. Indeed, I've guessed Mahiya's age because the Hadza only have a vague idea of how old they are. They don't keep track of years, days or hours. Time neither guides nor restricts them. It is believed that the Hadza language traditionally didn't have words for specific numbers past two, skipping onto a word for 'many' instead. Although researchers can't be sure, it seems that individual numbers higher than that have been absorbed from other dialects only recently.

This morning, like all the days I've spent with the Hadza, had a sense of freedom and variety. No day is the same, free as they are from schedules and deadlines. As such, they seem to have something we've lost. Despite the dangers and challenges, they seem free from worry. They appear either fully engaged in their activities or completely at ease as they relax together. Perhaps this is partly because they have few social rules to conform to, no social or self-imposed pressure of expectation to stress them out, no unnecessary possessions, jobs, household chores or social media. Without a sense of comparison or competition and no rush, they are living in the moment, the ultimate connoisseurs in mindfulness. There is no need even for leaders or chiefs or any specialists in the tribe – they all just contribute and enjoy doing so. And why wouldn't they – their adventurous lives are playful and enjoyable. They are free to live adventurously. Of course, I don't want to rose-tint the experience. Their world is also dangerous and for many short, with infant and child mortality high. But the feeling of *being alive* is so prevalent that just spending time in their company is like being wrapped in vitality. It is this freedom that has captivated me and made me feel so deeply privileged to get to experience the primal joy that this way of living offers.

For me, the childlike abandon of running free through the African bush was followed by a return to the office at the BBC. I spent several weeks in Africa, followed by several weeks typing up my notes, making recommendations and plans. For thirteen years, I worked in adventure and wildlife television as a researcher, producer and safety adviser, specialising in survival shows (with, for example, Bear Grylls, Ray Mears and Chris Ryan), remote wildlife films (even working with my hero David Attenborough once) and plenty of adventure challenge series, such as *Beyond Boundaries*. (Working as a freelancer meant I could keep my expedition leading going on the side.) I spent half my time working in the wilderness on adventures as an expedition leader or adventure filmmaker and half my time back in the UK doing 'normal' civilised stuff in the office or edit suite. I enjoyed the juxtaposition, but I often remember feeling like my 'life' happened when I was out having adventures, not sat in front of a screen. At the very least, my office-bound work was work, and my adventure-based work was a combination of work and play. I was grateful for this variety, because I know for many, perhaps for the majority, this is not the case.

One thing I was sure of was that there was a kind of joy I could not find in 'normal' life, a joy I could only experience if I crossed the threshold into another world. I believe one of the main reasons for this is because we have made work into toil; we've taken the fun out of what we spend most of our time doing. For many today, work tends to be something we do in exchange for economic reward. We do the work, we get paid, and that payment then enables us to satisfy our basic needs and, if we're lucky, gratify us with the stuff we want to buy or the activities we actually want to do. But it's different for nomadic hunter-gatherer tribes, whose economic system is founded on equality, on sharing and on cooperation. For the Hazda, work doesn't seem like toil: it's varied, it's educational and it's playful. It is still essential for survival, but it is also its own reward. While hunting and gathering does generate a reward at the end of it – the prize of food earnt as a result of those activities – the reward also comes from the *doing* part. The adventure of hunting and gathering, as well as the social engagement in doing it with friends and family, are the rewards.

Play has become a way of being, which stems from how they are brought up. The Hadza children are educated through play. They play at hunting and gathering, at tool making, defending themselves from predators, at caring for and nursing each other, at negotiating and hut building. As adults, their work is simply an extension of that play as their skill levels increase and their playful activities become productive ones. Play, in a way, turns into work, yet it remains playful because it is so varied and is not burdensome nor even obligatory – members of the tribe can opt to join a hunt or not on any particular day. Furthermore, it requires a great deal of skill in order to rise to the challenges inherent in the wild, which brings with it feelings of achievement and self-efficacy. As such, the tribes people are fully engaged in what they are doing. Hunting or gathering is essentially one big team treasure hunt.

While in Tanzania, I also spent several days with the Hadza women gathering, which involved mostly digging with sticks to find tubers. They moved slowly between foraging grounds; the air was filled with chatter and the occasional shriek of laughter. Mothers with babies joined the group but didn't feel the need to be productive; they were there for the gossip. I couldn't speak the language, but I knew what was happening: here was a group of women hanging out, just shooting the breeze. There was no rush, expectation or worry; it did not look or feel like 'work'. This echoes what Alf Wannenburgh described in his book *The Bushmen* about the Ju/'hoansi tribe: 'In our experience all of the gathering expeditions were jolly events. With the [Ju/'hoansi's] gift of converting chores into social occasions, they often had something of the atmosphere of a picnic outing with children.'

As well as being sociable, varied and, to a degree, optional, hunter-gatherers' work is also skill-intensive but not labour-intensive. It's hard to put a figure on exactly how long a foraging individual invests in work, but anthropologists have observed between fifteen to forty hours per week. In between short bursts of varied work, they play games, make musical instruments, dance, sing, relax and chat, the kind of thing the rest of us do when we're on holiday. It's ironic that despite having invented countless labour-saving devices, we spend much more time working than our ancestors, and that work is less playful and social.

The Hadza and other hunter-gatherer tribes don't have words for 'being happy' over the long-term, only for current emotions, such as 'joy' or 'sadness'. They are present-oriented to meet current needs rather than future-based ones. This is generally at odds with how we tend to work in the Western world. Our reward comes at the end: we work for pay day, rather than for enjoyment of the work itself (with the exception of those fortunate enough to truly love what they do). Ever since the first farmers planted seeds for future harvest, everything seems to have become future-oriented in some way. We work hard at school to get into college or university, so that we can get a job, so that we can buy our dream house/car/life and get a sufficient pension. Putting off happiness for the promise of it another day would not be something a hunter-gatherer would understand.

The problem with this future-based approach is that it doesn't always work in our favour. Apart from the rather morbid old chestnut that 'you could get knocked over by a bus tomorrow', there is a more scientific reason to live for the moment. The attitude of 'I can't be happy until ... I get the promotion ... I find the right partner ... I achieve this or that goal' can actually stop you from living a joyful life today. We hold ourselves hostage to the notion that the grass is greener and that our life is incomplete without that promotion/partner/goal, so we do not allow ourselves to feel grateful for what we have right in front of us. Worse than that, once we get the thing we've been sacrificing ourselves for, our expectations have risen in line with our desires, so we do not necessarily feel any happier, or the feeling is only transitory. In a report called 'The Biology of Happiness' in the *Science and Society Journal*, researchers found that our emotional response to pleasant stimuli weakens or completely ceases if a stimulus remains constant (a 'new' phone, for example, is only new for so long). Positive emotions serve as a lure to engage in certain behaviours (like the excitement of opening the box, pulling out your shiny new phone, showing off to your friends), but these feelings cease once the need or want driving them has been satisfied (there's now a newer phone on the market; the promotion is now the job; Mr Right is now Mr Everyday). The satisfaction has worn off, but the memory of the pleasant moment remains, and we want to experience it again. This phenomenon is called 'the hedonic treadmill' by psychologists, because once that novelty wears off, we want to gain that pleasurable feeling again, so we keep striving for more, rather than focusing on feeling grateful for what we already have. We are forever chasing happiness but never holding on to it.

Chasing happiness while missing what is in front of you is a hard habit to break. For all of my twenties and into my thirties, I was focused on climbing the career ladder, putting off pleasure today in order to get a promotion tomorrow, to impress others in order to hide my self-doubt and to feel that I was 'doing OK' by society's measures. We evolved to adapt to ever-changing environments and opportunities, to live playfully, adaptively and most of all adventurously. Yet our growing need to have more, be more, do more has made us less satisfied. Thankfully, I found some balance through adventure. Being able to switch regularly between 'normal' life and my 'adventure' work saved my sanity. Without escaping from time to time to challenge myself in novel environments, I would probably have broken. And that is why I'm so sure that adventure is the antidote to the society we've created. The variety, novelty, engagement and uncertainty of adventure are such important factors in inducing joy. We can't go back to being hunter-gatherers to experience these joy-inducing feelings, but we can find them in the adventures that we opt to take part in. Of course, there are other ways to experience these stimuli and emotions. If we can find work that is playful by nature – sufficiently varied, unpredictable and adventurous – we can bring more joy to our working lives. If we can let go of the modern requirement to bring everything under control, to eliminate risk, uncertainty and hardship in favour of comfort, certainty and ease, we can replace monotony with joy, and enjoy now more. But adventurous activity is the most natural fit, because it's what we and our ancestors evolved to do.

Adventure is also immersive, mentally and physically; you can get lost in the activity because you are so absorbed in it. This engagement is one of the components of wellbeing (as discussed in chapter two), so the more engaged we are in the activities we participate in, the better. When we improve the quality of our experiences, we improve our enjoyment of life itself. And adventure can provide the ultimate opportunity for complete engagement, when we are so immersed in an activity that we lose track of time and find a sense of flow. Flow is a concept describing those moments when you're completely absorbed in a challenging but doable task. Athletes, musicians, writers and artists can find themselves in the flow 'zone' when they have learnt the appropriate skills and an ability to exercise control and gain feedback; this enables them to be confident enough to participate and stretch themselves fully. We can all find flow through adventure as we become so absorbed in what we're doing that we lose track of time, forget our everyday worries and let go of self-consciousness or fear and just engage.

The Hungarian psychologist Mihaly Csikszentmihalyi discovered that flow can bring deep joy and satisfaction; in his words, 'the best moments in our lives are not the passive, receptive, relaxing times. The best moments usually occur if a person's body or mind is stretched to its limits in a voluntary effort to accomplish something difficult and worthwhile'. Learning new skills is good for our sense of self-esteem, self-efficacy and therefore our mood. Mastering the skill of helming downwind (steering a sailing boat powered by the full force of the wind) or nailing a difficult climbing route can lead to a boost in how we feel about ourselves and an increase in how engaged we feel in the activity itself, whereas a lack of progress can lead to despondency. Pushing through our comfort zone, rising to challenges and persisting brings the reward of entering the flow zone, when you've mastered something you previously found challenging and lose yourself in the activity.

Generally, the joy and gratification people gain from activities in which flow is possible means they will do that activity regardless of cost or risk, regardless of what they gain from doing it, just because they love to do it and feel completely absorbed in it. 'Flow,' writes Mihaly, 'is the state in which people are so involved in an activity that nothing else seems to matter; the experience itself is so enjoyable that people will do it even at great cost, for the sheer sake of doing it.' Indeed, researchers into adventure sport have found that flow is one of the primary motivators for participation rather than being hooked on adrenaline, as previously thought.

Until recently, the common perception was that there was something deviant about high-risk extreme-sport lovers, such as big-wave surfers, BASE jumpers and free-solo rock climbers. But, as Eric Brymer has discovered, 'the traditional approach is flawed'. A huge amount of training, preparation and effort goes into participating in extreme sports successfully. So, realising there must be a more significant pull than simply being hooked on adrenaline, Brymer set out to research the topic and has, consequently, been able to bust the myth of the adrenaline junkie. He found that what we're drawn to is the deep engagement felt in the heart of the action of the extreme task, after fear has quietened down and before the feeling of empowerment that stays with you afterwards. Eric has found that 'that quiet period is what people tell me is the real reason why they go back'.

These moments of quiet bliss appear to be the result of flow but also of peak experiences. Psychologist Abraham Maslow developed the concept of peak experiences, which are described as altered states of consciousness characterised by euphoria and the moment of reaching one's full potential. Maslow considered them to be one of the most important goals in life, because they are the moments when you feel your true self. Flow is an internal process that is enjoyable but short-lived, whereas peak experiences leave us seeing ourselves and the world in a more positive way.

According to Brymer, 'climbers, BASE jumpers, kayakers, all talk about floating – being at one with the environment', which is strongly connected to a feeling of freedom. In his 2013 study about why people do extreme sports, Brymer's results identified 'six elements of freedom [including] freedom from constraints, freedom as movement, freedom as letting go of the need for control'. One participant, a BASE jumper, described it as 'defying gravity, and I define gravity as all things that pull you down in life, you know, everyday living'.

One of the things nearly everyone I interview about adventure mentions eventually is that they feel 'alive' or 'most alive' doing adventure. I hear the phrase 'most alive' so commonly I almost don't notice it now, but of course that's why it's so important. 'Feeling alive' was the common theme Brymer also discovered from his research – that extreme-sport participants are drawn to it because of 'this notion of coming home, a way of being authentic and true to yourself, of living the person you are inside'. In this way, extreme sports are not deviant but celebrant. They're not about hedonism but about commitment to life itself. They're not about adrenaline addiction or risking death but about opti-mising living.

As such, couldn't we start to perceive adventure not as the pursuit of some kind of death wish only undertaken by adrenaline junkies, but the pursuit of feeling alive? The adventurers I've met are life addicts – addicted to the feeling of living life to the full. As Brymer has noted, 'It's a flourish-ing, an opportunity to realize our potential as human beings.'

Sadly, the traditional, stereotypical narratives of the danger-loving adrenaline junkie may partly be to blame for the absence of adventurous activities in mainstream wellbeing initiatives, despite so much research demonstrating that adventurers are better equipped to cope with and enjoy life. Arguably, extreme and adventure sports might even be more useful than traditional interventions for encouraging lifelong wellness and adaptability.

Laura Slavin, a mountain biker known for her gap-jumping free-ride skills, agrees. Like her fellow extreme-adventure-sport enthusiasts, she sees flying through the air on her bike as freedom. Slavin told *Bicycling* magazine in 2019, 'It's total immersion in a moment in a way that I've had a hard time ever getting from anywhere else.' As soon as she first experienced that joyful and peaceful feeling, she knew she'd found her 'thing'. She hadn't been athletic up until this point, but when a friend took her to a bike park and she 'caught a foot of air, I've never been more thrilled and excited and happy in my whole life'. Subsequently, Laura began going to the bike park every week, looking for the joy of the jump, and did so many laps her friends said it was her 'hamster wheel'. Except for Slavin, unlike the hedonic treadmill, it wasn't the promise of more stuff or greater success she was seeking; it was that joyful experience, that feeling of freedom and flow, that she got from experiencing 'air'.

In adventure, joy isn't always experienced in the moment. With the hardships one can face on adventures, sometimes joy is experienced retrospectively, when we look back at the suffering we persevered through and realise it was, despite it all, still fun. That sense of achievement can generate immense joy. Amongst the adventure community in Britain, it's got its own name: it's called 'type-two fun'. Type-one fun is the kind that is enjoyable at the time and afterwards, whereas type-two fun is not enjoyable at the time but is in retrospect. Adventure is full of type-two fun. Indeed, there's not an adventure I've been on that hasn't involved it to some degree.

I experienced type-two fun on a racing yacht in a hurricane in the middle of the Atlantic Ocean in 2012. I was filming a round-the-world race for the BBC. I'd never been on a sailing boat before, but the BBC had just sent me on a two-week sailing course. Most of the crew had bonded during months at sea together, but I was replacing a cameraman who'd been disgraced and thrown off the boat. They understandably didn't have positive feelings about TV crew. I was tasked with directing, filming, recording sound and backing up the footage. These jobs are usually shared between a small team, but there was only one berth on the boat, so I'd have to do it all. To begin with, filming was challenging, but once we hit bad weather, which was most of the time, the effort needed was tremendous. A racing yacht keels over at an angle when at speed, which means you spend most of your time hanging off one or other sides of the boat, or wedged into a corner. If you let go, you risk tumbling off. Add to this hurricane-force winds, rain and sea spray, all while I was trying to record pictures and sound on expensive electronic equipment while hanging off a moving climbing frame and being hosed with water. Sometimes in the dark. And while trying not to get washed into the sea and lost.

The weather was so rough that the majority of the crew were seasick – for a while we were very worried that one young woman would have to be evacuated, as she was no longer able to keep any fluid down. And if we'd hit a piece of flotsam or jetsam while racing at this speed, which would have been unavoidable in these big waves, it would have torn a hole in the hull.

The journey should have been a nightmare, and I admit I was pushed to my limit at times. But it was an experience I wouldn't have missed for the world, including the suffering – because of the suffering. Under my foulies (wet-weather gear), I found myself beaming much more often than despairing. There is a singular feeling of exhilaration in flying along in the open ocean, pushed by the power of the wind, under the light of a full moon so bright you can pick out the details on the deck. These unique moments were earnt in part through the suffering. And even the awful times themselves – the frequent unpleasantness of leaving the warmth and putting on wet clothes to face the cold on deck or the bolt of fear I felt when the boat tipped over so far that the mast nearly got caught in the sea (which would have violently capsized the boat) – would take on new meaning eventually. Having been in a similarly tough position before, I could expect that however bad it got, as long as we all got home in one piece, even the low moments would give me a source of satisfaction and joy in the future. And, of course, through this adversity I made a life-long friend, Emma, and we laugh more now about the tough times onboard than we do the easier days at sea.

During the Atlantic crossing, I was reminded of something a Norwegian climber had told me years before: 'The English are the best at suffering.' I'd smiled because it was true: while my life had been a series of adventures, it had also been a series of 'sufferfests' of type-two fun. From the horizontal rain hitting us in the face like bullets that we endured on Dartmoor to the pain of walking on raw blisters in Alaska or through the searing heat of the Taklamakan Desert (the name translates as 'you go in, but you don't come out' in the local Uyghur language), those moments are when I've felt most alive, and my perseverance has brought about a retrospective joy.

Embracing this kind of joy shows not just the grit but the optimistic nature exhibited by many adventurers. The monotonous hours hiking up yet another slope with a false summit (a peak that appears to be the pinnacle of the mountain but upon reaching it, it turns out the summit is higher), wading through chest-deep snow or cutting through dense, insect-filled undergrowth, the effort just to make one kilometre of progress, the sort of progress you'd make in the time it takes to drink a cup of tea on a good day. This is type-two fun. Type-one fun leads to celebratory beers; after type two, you just need a drink.

Yet, by the time you are sat around the campfire at base camp or sharing stories with the family back home, this sufferfest has transformed in your memory to a defining moment in your life. Either the worst bits fade and become a little rose-tinted or the very worst part of the experience gives you the biggest pleasure.

For a time, I did wonder whether this masochistic mindset was abnormal – enjoying an activity that is painful or tedious is surely a bit twisted? But then I realised that it was fun because it was purposeful. Type-two fun is joyful afterwards because there is a payoff, an experience you wouldn't have had or a discovery you wouldn't have made without the suffering attached. Reaching that summit, getting to camp and kicking off those boots – the relief and the sense of achievement after enduring what you have – that's what cultivates the feeling of joy.

As such, adventure offers two types of joy – the retrospective joy of type-two fun, which comes from the deep sense of purposeful achievement of having 'made it through', and the pure immersed-in-the-moment joy of type-one fun, which comes from deeply engaging in the activity and finding a sense of freedom and flow. Both generate golden memories – and both types of joy cause adventurers to go back for more, time and time again. Both are part of the hunter-gatherer's daily existence, too. It's in our DNA; we're wired to seek out both sorts of joy and to thrive when we find them.

Ten

To Find Meaning

'You must go on adventures to find out where you belong.'
Sue Fitzmaurice, author

Like a lot of people, pre-adventure Stu Skinner had trouble finding meaning in his life. He struggled with manic depression, and after his best friend died by suicide at twenty-one, Stu also tried to take his own life. He survived, but things still weren't good. He'd lost his job as a result of the suicide attempt. He'd lost his best friend. And then he lost a long-term relationship. Aged twenty-six, Stu felt like his life was over, and he just couldn't see a way out from his despair. But then a friend asked him to cycle 3,000 miles across Asia with him. With nothing left to lose, Stu agreed to go on an adventure – one that would ultimately change and perhaps save his life.

I met Stu in 2019 when I was researching mental health first aid training for adventurers. Increasingly, adventure leaders are managing serious mental illness in their groups, including self-harm, eating disorders, depression and anxiety. The standard mental health first aid courses available are fine for those working in areas where an ambulance might be there within minutes, but they aren't good enough for leaders who might find themselves days from help with a person suffering a severe episode. I wanted Explorers Connect to be one of the first organisations in the world to offer remote mental health first aid training courses, enabling the instructors to better support those in their charge. Stu had the perfect mix of experience outdoors and in teaching mental health first aid, and as we discussed what such a bespoke course might look like, he revealed to me why he does what he does.

He explained that cycling across Asia was the most difficult journey of his life, but it was worth it because it had given him a future. At first, it was his faith in humanity that was restored after strangers rallied to help him after he was hit by a bus in Cambodia and flew over the bonnet. 'Lots of people came to my aid,' Stu said. 'People put antiseptic cream on my wounds, another poured water on my face, someone bandaged me up, another drove me to hospital. All these people, complete strangers, helped me.' This was reinforced when Stu and his friend made it to the highest point of the Philippines, having cycled over incredibly rough terrain: children ran out of their villages and began pushing their bicycles, helping them upwards.

When Stu reached the top of that mountain, in that moment, he knew he could get his life sorted. Standing on that summit also gave him perspective about what he'd been through. He explained that 'summitting mountains represented the struggle I'd been through. The struggle to get out of my house, the struggle to work in a coffee shop because I wanted to beat my social anxiety, the struggle to get out of bed on the difficult days.' He could give himself credit for this achievement – for embarking on a journey that had taken him from negative thinking to allowing positive thoughts in. Adventure had given him the proof he needed that there was always the possibility of a brighter future out there. Knowing what is possible, what can be achieved, had given him hope and purpose: 'There are always positives from the darkest experiences, it's just whether or not we choose to see them; that's the wisdom that came from the trip.' Back in England, he hadn't seen any future for himself and had almost given up hope, but here he was on top of a mountain filled with hope once more and glad to be alive.

Stu's future included many more challenges, and each one demonstrated what was possible. He walked across the USA and completed the Appalachian Trail as part of his continued self-therapy. Taking on challenges had given Stu's life purpose. But now his challenges were more important than ever: 'I realised I could inspire others to do the same.' Stu had set up a charity to help others who were in the position he'd found himself in. He now worked as both a mental-health adviser and an expedition leader. Since that first adventure, Stu had led fifty expeditions and trained hundreds in mental health first aid. He was living a meaningful life, one where he was helping young people with mental-health issues to discover what he had discovered: adventure can give your life purpose and hope. That is the dual-pronged effect that adventure can have on people. First, it can give your days a sense of purpose, then as you embark on more adventures, you build on that meaning making each challenge more significant.

That's also what happened for Alex Staniforth. He joined me to share his story at an Explorers Connect gathering in Bristol in 2018. Many people feel like they're climbing a mountain long before they climb an actual mountain, and this was the case for Alex. As a child he was afraid to be left alone for fear of having an epileptic seizure. He'd throw phones across the room in frustration about his stammer and suffered from panic attacks. As a result of verbal and physical bullying, he was devoid of self-confidence and felt worthless.

In 2008, at the age of thirteen, Alex tried paragliding on holiday in Turkey. 'It felt ecstatic,' Alex said. 'I was so scared, but I had never felt so free. It was amazing.' That was the start of his journey, unearthing his passion for the outdoors. Scuba diving, rock climbing, mountain biking and running followed as Alex was keen to discover what else he could master: 'I came home with a new mindset. I wanted to try different things. I wanted to keep challenging myself. It was like having a new lease of life. After epilepsy had held me back, stopped me dreaming, I now had a confidence to try things again.' He actively sought adventurous challenges, that first adventure paving the way for the next. A Ben Nevis climb led to a Lake District walk, which led to the Three Peaks Challenge before climbing Mont Blanc at seventeen and heading to the Himalayas for the first time aged eighteen to climb Baruntse (7,129 metres): 'The first thing I noticed was that I could handle my anxiety better. I felt fitter and stronger and more capable, my resilience increasing after each trip.'

For both Stu and Alex, adventure became a way to cope, a way to prove their capabilities. The stammer and panic attacks were ongoing, but Alex explained, 'I've got better at managing them, and now I never let them become a barrier. Adventure has become my therapy and purpose. It has become a way to overcome challenges in life, not just outdoors but also in work and relationships. It's been about self-discovery, because I discovered where I belonged and who I was, where I could feel good about myself. And it made me feel so much more able and resilient.' Not only was it a way to fight back from epilepsy, bullying and self-doubt, adventure also gave Alex a continual purpose in life. Rather than victimhood defining him, adventure now did.

As we've already seen, thanks to our fear of failure, the hardest part of adventure is starting. But failing not only teaches us valuable lessons about how not to do things next time, it also gives us a chance to question our purpose and to find the meaning in what we're doing. In 2014, at the age of nineteen, Alex attempted his biggest mountain yet, Everest, but it ended in disaster with an avalanche that tragically killed sixteen people. He returned the following year but was trapped on the mountain with his team when a huge earthquake struck Nepal and devastated the country, taking the lives of three teammates at base camp: 'I've failed Everest twice, but I'm glad I failed, because it gave me a chance to question my purpose and gave me a chance to change my *why.*' For Alex, his purpose from adventuring was threefold: it was therapy, as outdoor challenges became a way to overcome his internal ones; it was a confidence booster, because outdoor adventures made him realise he could do more than he had thought; and it was a source of energy, making him want to achieve things in life and embrace his difference: 'I wasn't trying to fit into the crowd anymore. I didn't want to be like everyone else. I was proud to be different.' It also gave him the means to make a difference in the world. 'Making a difference for good causes in the process of adventure is very important to me,' said Alex, whose early charity fundraising led to the honour of being a London 2012 Olympic Torchbearer through Chester at the age of seventeen.

Alex's experience on Everest left him more determined to make an even bigger difference. He began fundraising for Nepal by cycling the height of Everest in one day (known as Everesting) and organising Walk4Nepal on the anniversary of the earthquake, which has raised more than £40,000 to date for PHASE Worldwide to support the earthquake victims. Now Alex is an ambassador for YHA England & Wales and Ordnance Survey, which gives him the opportunity to reach and inspire more people to also find meaning through adventure. In 2019, he co-founded the charity Mind Over Mountains to support others in restoring their mental health through outdoor experiences.

Alex realised he didn't want Everest enough any more, because he could make a bigger and more rewarding difference closer to home. 'Everest was just one step on my journey,' Alex said. 'Now I want to use that journey to inspire others to overcome their own Everest in life – because the biggest obstacle will always be ourselves.' Alex realised that the purpose was more important than the place. So, he embarked on a new challenge called Climb the UK, which would see him climbing to the highest point of all 100 counties in the United Kingdom: 'The *why* became more important than the summit, which is why Climb the UK became the priority; it was my own thing. It was purely down to my own physical and mental ability to achieve the goal, rather than things outside of my control.'

Alex understands the meaning and significance of every part of his life and how the adversities he faced in childhood led him towards adventure and then to making a difference in the world. Those difficult times acted as a catalyst for choosing to live a more adventurous and purposeful life: 'If it wasn't for the bullying and self-doubt, I wouldn't have been compelled to find this path toward achieving my potential.' And later, following the tragedies Alex experienced while on his Everest attempts, the renewed sense of gratitude made his path in life, and life itself, feel even more meaningful and significant. Indeed, these tragic events made Alex appreciate more and complain less: 'It takes a lot to phase me in everyday life now ... People complain about the bus being late, but that doesn't matter. Just like our flight being cancelled for our holiday to Iceland. My family were saying what a nightmare it was, but I had a renewed sense of perspective and thought, So what? We don't always choose the challenges we face – but we can choose how we respond to them.'

And adventure can be the most meaningful response of all. As was true for Alan Creedon. His adventure started with a sole purpose: to raise funds in memory of his sister. But it ended up with him finding meaning and a fresh purpose in life: to help people connect more deeply with the great outdoors.

Alan contacted me in 2015 through the Explorers Connect free 'Join A Team' networking service I run that helps people realise their adventure dreams by linking up would-be adventurers and potential support teams. Alan needed someone to help him get across the Irish Sea in a kayak, having only been in one once before in his life. His heartfelt but audacious request was answered by a generous and highly experienced kayaker called Mike Alexander, who ended up making Alan's adventure plans a reality. Grateful for the small part I had played in their introduction, Alan told me about the meaning of the expedition several months later once he'd returned home.

Alan explained that five years earlier he had lost his sister Aoife. She'd been born severely brain damaged and couldn't walk, talk or communicate in the ways most people could. She had suffered with cerebral palsy and had pneumonia five times as a baby. The full-time care Aoife needed was hard on Alan's family. As a child, he was confused and sad: 'My whole family was sad about our situation, but we got on with it, without really talking about it.' After Aoife died, Alan, who was now in his forties and father to his own kids, still felt a lot of the pain he had felt as a child and believed he needed to do something to pay tribute to his sister's life. So, he decided to walk. His walk would take him from Manchester, where he'd spent the last twenty years, to Dingle in Ireland, where he had spent his first twenty years: 'I had never done such a thing before, nor had I any idea of how I would cross the Irish sea – I just knew I wanted to do it differently. I also decided to raise a chunk of money for charity. That was the premise.'

Six months later, Alan set off from his house in Manchester, waving goodbye to his wife and daughter as he hit the road for his twenty-nine-day hike. He had trained in the months before, but it was the first time in his life that he'd had to get fit for something. The memory of his sister, and the idea that he would raise loads of money for charity, worked as great 'excuses' to help motivate him: 'I had always worked hard at different jobs, and I had always done a half-arsed job of looking after what I needed for myself. This journey helped me change all that. And I suffered on that journey. Boy, did I suffer!'

By day two, Alan was practically crippled with huge blisters on the soles of his feet. For the following seven days, he walked on painful, pulsing blisters, having to sing out loud at times to distract himself from the pain. 'It certainly kept the cows entertained,' Alan said, laughing. He was also grateful for the help and support along the way when people would offer him a bed or help him with his backpack: 'I felt no shame accepting help, because we all knew my journey was bigger than me.' Alan's family also rallied to help support his journey, helping out with places to stay, with fundraising and being there for him when he needed encouragement.

In the spring of 2016, Alan stepped into a double sea kayak and set off across the Irish Sea from Porth Dafarch, near Holyhead. At the time, he had no idea it would be twenty-two gruelling hours before he set foot on land again, in Dun Laoghaire, Dublin. That part of his journey changed his life for ever and opened the door to new experiences and a deep awareness that now drives him to live the meaningful life he had always wanted to.

'Crossing the Irish sea was a tremendous feat,' Alan said. Mike Alexander had answered his call, providing the kayak, expertise and guidance Alan needed so he could get going, but that was just the start: 'In the twenty-two hours crossing the sea, I was confronted by pain, fatigue and, of course, the intense beauty and charm of the sea. On the sixty-mile crossing, I had sea sickness for three hours. We encountered some choppy seas, hallucinations and confusion due to lack of sleep, misleading lights, ferries and other ships, and a whale even came and checked us out.' When they reached Ireland, Mike caught the ferry back home, and Alan went for a well-deserved rest. Alan then walked the remaining 230 miles to his hometown, and despite torn ligaments and a metatarsal stress fracture in one of his feet, he pressed on, all the way to Dingle: 'Through the course of that journey, I overcame obstacles the likes of which I would never have otherwise tackled, found myself in pain, lonely, ecstatic, challenged, powerful, even superhuman at times, and I exceeded all my own expectations of myself.' Alan also raised more than £21,000 for mental health and disability charities – his initial purpose fulfilled.

However, as is often the case with adventure, the walk ended up being about more than raising funds for charity in his sister's honour. It also gave Alan the space he needed to work through what had been holding him back: 'I improved my relationship with my family, understood myself better, and put to rest many of the grudges and petty issues I had been holding on to regarding my sister's life and death. I allowed myself to grieve through taking action and tackling my problems head on. I would really recommend adventure for this. Through challenging myself in ways I was not used to and taking risks I would otherwise not have taken, I changed my perspective and became more open to the world around me. I gained massive perspective from the people I met who shared amazing and humbling stories of joy and suffering from their own lives. I spent quality time outdoors in nature, connecting with the land and sea and having that space around me to reflect on my life. Most of all, I gave myself the chance, in this short life, to step outside "normal" activities and give myself the time to begin to work out what I actually wanted for myself rather than what I thought society expected of me.' After that journey, Alan moved to Italy with his family to have the quality of life he longed for, living in the mountains, growing his own food and spending more time in nature. He also undertook training to become a nature guide, helping others to deepen their connection to the outdoors and find meaning outside of 'normal' life.

Not only had adventure helped Alan to achieve his fund-raising purpose, it had helped him to feel like his actions, responses and contributions were meaningful, and adventure also provided the catalyst for him to find the meaningful life he'd been dreaming of living.

So, what is it about adventure that gives life meaning? There are a number of answers to this. First, adventure gives you a direction in which to travel, a purpose and hope for the future. Second, adventure places our responses to situations centre stage – we notice how we respond to challenges, which also demonstrates how our actions have value and significance. Third, when we live our lives with a sense of intention, to live adventurously, to contribute, to raise funds as part of our expeditions, that's living a life with meaning. And, finally, it is through adventure that we can give what has happened to us in the past meaning, too. For Stu, Alex and Alan, their adversities became meaningful after they'd embarked on adventure. They used what they'd endured in life to spur them on and, consequently, to inspire and teach others.

Adventure gives us a sense that we have control over our own lives. Circumstances may have dealt us a difficult hand, but by cutting our own trail and showing ourselves what we're capable of, we can seize control of how we respond and live our lives. This sense of responsibility is what keeps us alive when we face danger. Adventure forces you to take responsibility, unlike modern life. And this responsibility, this autonomy, makes life feel more meaningful, because we are choosing our response.

Stu, Alex and Alan chose their own responses to adversity, which gave their lives fresh meaning, empowering them and all those they inspire through their purposeful work. The knock-on effect has been happier and more joyful lives, not just despite adversity but because of it. Surviving adversity gave them more power over their futures. For had they not faced the challenges life threw at them, they wouldn't be the people they are today. So, although they struggled initially, their adversities led them towards adventure, and adventure gave them the coping skills to rise to those challenges and come out the other side feeling better and living more meaningful lives. For Stu, Alex, Alan, and so many more of us, an adventurous life provides the platform for a life well-lived, a happy life, a meaningful life.

Eleven

To Become Your Best You

'How we spend our days is, of course, how we spend our lives.'

Annie Dillard, author

I hope, having read this far, that the many benefits – physical, psychological, social and otherwise – to making adventurous activity a part of your life are now clear to you. The more we adventure, the more we are gifted with personal growth, resilience, wisdom and joy. By actively seeking challenges, choosing to face fear and uncertainty, engaging in adversity and risk, we get to feel really, truly, alive. When you wrap it all together, adventure is about becoming the best person you can be and living your best life.

Through the stories from my own life, the lives of those I've been fortunate enough to call fellow travellers and evidence drawn from a variety of scientific disciplines, we've learnt what adventure has the power to do and why it's something we should implement into our own lives and throughout our societies. We've learnt that we are built for adventure but our quest for comfort and progress has been getting in the way of living adventurously. This has created a mismatch between what our bodies and minds evolved to do and the lifestyles we have created. We've seen evidence for the detrimental effect an absence of adventure can have.

We've also discovered that adventurous activity can be the perfect antidote to the maladies of modern life by helping us to live healthier, less stressful and more engaging and authentic existences. We've learnt about the transformational power of adventure, the Adventure Effect, and how it helps us to think, feel and do better, leading us to optimal wellbeing. We've seen how it empowers us with the knowledge that we can do more than we thought we could. And we've learnt why pushing ourselves out of our comfort zone helps us to grow, to cope better and heal faster from whatever adversities life throws in our path. And how it brings us together in purpose and shared joy.

We now understand what's at stake, but we've also learnt what we need to do about it. As I said at the start of this book, I truly believe that adventure is a necessity of the human spirit and that *anyone* can do it. So, in a final call to action, we'll explore a variety of ways you can live more adventurously – how to add adventure to your life in simple ways, practical actions you can take today, tomorrow and beyond, so you can become your best self and live your best and 'most alive' life.

Adventure is for everyone

Adventure doesn't have to be monumental; you don't have to climb Everest. To kick-start a more adventurous lifestyle, you might simply take small adventurous steps to test yourself in the natural arena. You could, for example:

- go for a run or a cycle somewhere new every couple of weeks
- hike, run or cycle a known route but do it under the cover of darkness
- explore a new area around your workplace on foot in your lunch break
- camp in your garden
- join a hiking, biking or kayaking club
- schedule an adventure weekend away from home every month
- take part in an organised adventure-challenge event

Contrary to popular belief, adventure is accessible to anyone of any age at any time and can fit into our busy working lives.

In 2010, my friend Tim Moss started his Everyday Adventures campaign, encouraging people to camp in their gardens or living rooms, take adventures in their lunchbreaks or go on mini excursions during evenings after work. It arose out of the increasing difficulty that he and other 'big adventurers' he knew were having in keeping their big adventures going. The problems were due to unending battles for funding, lifestyle changes such as having children, and wanting to reduce their environmental footprint.

I knew Tim through the RGS, and for some time, until he moved out of the area, he hosted the Explorers Connect gatherings in London. Tim had always been passionate about helping others adventure by reinforcing the idea that 'you really don't need time, money or expertise to have an adventure'. The campaign might have been a surprise to some people, given that Tim was an accomplished explorer – he had organised expeditions to all seven continents, made first and first-British ascents of several mountains, from Russia to Bolivia, and travelled around the world using eighty different methods of transport. Yet he described it as 'one of the best things I've done'.

In 2011, another friend, Alastair Humphreys, coined the phrase 'microadventure' to promote the idea that adventures can be small and achievable, in particular by squeezing them into the 5 p.m. to 9 a.m. slot, around busy working days. A classic microadventure might involve climbing a hilltop, a short cycle or train ride away, taking only a bivvy bag to sleep in rather than a tent, and making it back to the office, shirt and tie in place, in time for a 9 a.m. start the following morning. In 2012, Alastair was nominated for the National Geographic Adventurer of the Year award for his campaign to involve ordinary people in microadventures.

Meanwhile, I was having my own epiphany. Having spent my life and career travelling around the globe in search of adventure, I was now running an adventure community, the first of its kind before Facebook, Meetup and other social-media sites took the lead. At Explorers Connect, my initial aim was to bring the expedition community together to help others live adventurously. However, until then, my idea of adventure had revolved around far-flung places. My life had been defined by taking myself on bigger and bigger challenges, with the space in between simply marking time until the next expedition. Yet, I was encountering the same problems as other 'big adventurers'. In my head, adventure was something that needed time, money and planning. It was to be waited, saved and planned for.

Tim and Al's ideas were refreshing, but it was my community that ultimately pushed me to challenge my assumptions. Amongst the dizzying summits, continental crossings and polar conquests, the community kept asking me to arrange smaller adventures so that we could meet up more regularly. At first, I pushed back. But I run huge international expeditions, I'd arrogantly tell myself. I didn't want to arrange a kayaking trip in Devon. But, of course, I was wrong. Eventually, I did arrange a kayaking trip in Devon, and it was wonderful. So wonderful in fact that I immediately arranged more. Within a couple of years, Explorers Connect went from being a hub for extreme adventurers to take on life-changing challenges at the ends of the earth to a community of normal people who wanted to take on life-changing challenges closer to home (as well as at the ends of the earth too!).

It was a real eye-opener as to how accessible adventure could be. I learnt that instead of spending half the year planning and dreaming about the next adventure, I could go on adventures all the time. Instead of leaving most of my loved ones behind for months at a time, I could involve them in the adventures. They were accessible for all. It redefined what adventure was for me and gave me a more adventurous state of mind and freedom to explore the possibility of going on adventures at any time. I didn't have to agonise over the environmental impact of my flights. I didn't have to wait – I could just go and do it, whenever, which meant I could also get a more regular 'hit' of my chosen drug. Until then, life had always seemed to be 'on hold' between my big overseas travels; now I could appreciate adventure every day, or at least every week. I could do what mattered most to me more often. And the effects on my wellbeing were still significant.

This notion of going on smaller and more frequent adventures also fits better with the idea of adventure not being a 'go-once-and-fix-everything experience', but more of a lifestyle choice, a conscious decision to live more adventurously. So, what does this actually mean? What can you really do that's on your doorstep? The ideas below are from small adventures I've taken groups on where I have seen significant positive wellbeing outcomes over a weekend, or even a day. They are wonderful ways to step into a more adventurous lifestyle before committing to doing something bigger.

- **Go on a human-powered journey** – set yourself a challenge to walk, cycle or kayak from A to B during a day or a weekend. Make sure the journey is new to you or that you do the same journey in a novel way each time. The excitement of exploring new areas is as primal as it gets. Then there's the fun of problem-solving along the way. If you don't make it and have to catch a bus or call for a taxi, that's OK; it's all part of the adventure. It's the stepping outside of your comfort zone and trying that's important, not the end point. And when you *do* make it to the destination, the feeling of exhilaration is second to none. Start small and keep it simple; the most important thing is that you give it a go. Self-propelled journeys are some of the most effective forms of adventure to improve wellbeing, because you are relying on yourself and feel a great sense of achievement as you journey, getting physically and tangibly closer to your goal. You also get to really focus on being in the moment with your adventuring team, which is also good for your wellbeing and your relationships.

- **Seek the sunset and sunrise** – the natural rhythm of the sun is something the majority of us take for granted, but sunsets and sunrises are breathtaking and can induce feelings of awe. Walking into the approaching darkness just as everyone else is settling in for the night or cycling into the sunrise gives a sense of extra excitement and challenge. Even following a route in the dark that is familiar to you in the daytime is a novel experience; you'll use different senses, and it will feel like a different world. It's a great way to experience real adventure and excitement with little planning or travel.

- **Learn a new skill** – there are so many new skills you can learn in the outdoors. From bushcraft and campcraft to technical skills, such as navigation or white-water kayaking. Book in with an instructor or teach yourself. The satisfaction gained from being brave enough to try, followed by the feelings of success when you start your first campfire, nail your first kayak roll or micro-navigate through the night results in a unique and authentic feeling of pride. Having new experiences demands that you learn new skills, and learning new skills make you feel accomplished.

- **Embrace bad weather** – there is a dramatic feeling and sense of camaraderie that bad weather creates, which can add an element of adventure to even the most regular of tasks. Bored of your usual running route? Rather than avoiding the rain and wind, choose to run in it. You will come back wet-through but invigorated, like a big kid playing outside in puddles, without a care in the world.

- **Sleep outside** – camping is always an adventure, no matter how many times you've done it, and spending nights outside is one of the simplest ways to live more adventurously. An easy start is to camp in your (or your friend's) garden. Once you progress further afield, try a wilderness campsite instead of a site that has all the modern conveniences and distractions. Immerse yourself in nature and the experience. Toast marshmallows and wake up to birdsong. Once you are feeling confident, try a bivvy bag instead of a tent, or try camping on your own instead of with friends, or in the wilderness. Spend the night in a place where you can see your city or town from high up. Ask a local farmer if you can camp on their hill (I've never been refused) or see if you can stay on top of a high building. See the lights come on as the sun goes down and watch the scene reveal itself from the darkness in the morning. You will feel more connected to your home and to those who've adventured with you.

- **Try parkour** – parkour is the physical discipline of moving freely over and through any terrain using only your body, principally through running, jumping and climbing. In practice, it is often about stepping outside of the limitations and rules of urban environments; for example, travelling via a wall or railing, rather than just the stairs. The railing becomes a slide as you learn to move via whatever route is possible. And that's key to the values of parkour: whatever the environment, everyone determines their own path. Parkour is often popular with people who are indifferent to traditional sports: it's non-competitive, there are few rules, so you can tap into your own creativity, and it's possible to practise in any terrain.

- **Try wild swimming** – all you need to pack is a swimming costume, a towel and an open mind. There are many wild-swimming communities and websites now that offer advice on locations, safety tips and organised events. Start in the summer, watch where others are swimming regularly, take a friend and walk in – don't jump into water you've not swum in before. If wild swimming seems a stretch too far, you could start with an alfresco swim in a lido.
- **Twenty-four-hour solo in the wilderness** – when you're alone you are completely reliant on your own abilities. It's scary, but it's also empowering. During the dozen youth development expeditions I've led, I've noticed that one of the most impactful elements has been the 'twenty-four-hour solo', which involves giving each young person their own space in the wilderness for a day and night. They are not given any tasks to do, except preparing meals and generally looking after themselves. And there are no rules, except that they are not to move more than a couple of minutes away from their campsite for safety reasons. I give them a radio, agree check-in times and emergency procedures and I also prowl around with binoculars, checking up on them at regular intervals. The young people are

understandably apprehensive, but it's always one of the most popular experiences of the expedition. Hearing how each person spent their time is a testimony to their authenticity as well as a lesson in empowerment. Lying alone under the stars, listening to the rain on canvas, spending their daylight hours with no external expectations, gives them time to reflect away from the noise of modern life. It is, of course, normal to be scared of going into the wilderness on your own, but don't let that stop you. No one should be denied this most natural freedom. Get sufficient training in campcraft and navigation, assess the risks and create a plan that you feel comfortable enough with in order to take that step and go into the wilderness alone.

- **Step outside of your comfort zone regularly** – once a month, ask yourself, When was the last time I stepped out of my comfort zone? When was the last time I did something new? And if it's been too long, commit to stretching yourself. Adventure is the perfect way to challenge yourself, because you're fully committed in body and mind.

And, finally, find like-minded friends. There's nothing more empowering than hanging out for an evening or a weekend with people who, when told about your adventure plans, will not say, 'Why would you want to do that?' but instead reply, 'That sounds awesome. I know a guy who can lend you a raft/tent/camel . . .' As long as you are surrounded by people who tell you that you can't do something or question your reasons for trying, you are going to find it much harder to start. That is why I set up Explorers

Connect, to link people and allow them to share opportunities and support each other and arrange their adventures. I believe that finding like-minded adventure teammates can be one of the most effective steps in starting and continuing to live more adventurously. I'd love you to join Explorers Connect but also other adventure communities. In the last few years, the multitude of adventure groups that have opened up on social-media sites such as Meetup and Facebook offer specialist gangs for those who want to wild swim, hike, canoe or learn bushcraft in your area, or groups for women, the LGBT community, people of specific ethnicities, people with disabilities or families. Another wonderful way of achieving this is to volunteer your time at an organisation that provides adventure as a form of development or therapy. You get to adventure and also see the benefits for others.

Big adventures

Small adventures come into their own if we want to take tentative first steps towards living more adventurously with fewer uncertainties, resources and risks. Regular, accessible adventure builds our confidence and step by step can help us to live more boldly. But small doses of adventure can also increase our ability to take on bigger challenges in life and also in the outdoors. I think there are times in all of our lives when we benefit most from committing to a big, challenging adventure. I have found that big adventures are particularly important at times of transition, at those crossroads when we either go with the flow or take action to define our next chapter ourselves.

That said, sometimes adventures, even big adventures, might not seem to work. I have led many overseas personal development expeditions to different parts of the globe, and although always impressed by the transformation most of the people have gone through at the time or shortly afterwards, there have been a handful who haven't seemed to have benefited when they returned home. This could have been because the expedition was not the right fit or that the impact was not yet visible, but I think there is another lesson to be learnt. I asked Dr Chris Loynes of the Institute for Science, Natural Resources and Outdoor Studies at the University of Cumbria why he thought adventure might not always work. He wisely suggested that there is a critical moment when we might fail these people. If they go on a transformational adventure of a lifetime and then return to their ordinary world but their peers, family, teachers, colleagues treat them the same as before, they might not be able to assimilate the benefits of the expedition into their normal lives. So, if you want to embark on adventure to experience true life transformation, it's important to prepare yourself for 're-entry' back into everyday life, rather than just going back to your old life, friends and situations without allowing for your changed mindset to take hold. For this reason, it's important to be aware of the potential for the adventure to be life-changing and let one or two people back home know so that they can accommodate those shifts. This is an important final step for all of us to incorporate into any adventure plan, but it also gave me an idea as to when big adventures might be at their most effective.

I have seen expeditions work best for young people who are going through great transitions in their lives, moving from school to further education or an apprenticeship, or from home to independent living. These explorers return with fresh appreciation of themselves and the world; they have reinvented themselves, and they can maintain this reinvention back in their everyday lives, because there is an expectation from those around them that they will have changed. It is an opportunity for sustained growth. The timing is right.

I've realised that these golden moments in our lives come about every so often, not just when children become adults. Whether it be a career change, a redundancy, getting married, getting divorced, a bereavement or becoming a parent, these huge, monumental shifts in our lives are times we need to rediscover and redefine ourselves in great leaps, and I believe this is when big adventures can be most effective. As our place in our ordinary world changes, adventure allows us to step into another world before returning to be the person we now wish to be. Adventure gives us the opportunity to reconnect with our sense of purpose, pursue our higher goals, heal and redefine ourselves. We can go through life conforming to the position in the community we find ourselves in or we can choose. Adventure empowers us but also gives us a space in which to evolve.

I have only recently come to understand that I have used big adventures at pivotal moments in my own life. To grow up, to grow into a new career, to strengthen relationships and to heal, but I've done this mostly by accident rather than design. However, for my next big adventure, I'm following my own advice. Becoming a parent is a life-altering step. We call our son the 'love bomb', because it's like a bomb has gone off in our lives, albeit a positive one. We're still in our own ordinary world, but our roles have completely changed. Our priorities, values and identities are challenged to the max. So, we've decided to go on an adventure together to become a family. No world records or extreme environments, but I'm as apprehensive, fearful and engaged as I have ever been of any big adventure, because we're treading new ground and giving ourselves the opportunity to step out of the everyday. We plan to walk the South West Coast Path, a national trail that goes from Minehead in Devon, to the northeast of us, before looping 630 miles south and then east around Cornwall to Poole Harbour in Dorset. We will do the walk in sections of days and weeks to fit around work and other commitments, so it will take years to complete, but we hope for it to work its magic as we take on an adventure together. We're aiming to make it to Dorset, but we know the real destination is to grow into a family. Taking on a big adventure does not mean you need to quit your job or save huge sums of money; even epic challenges can fit around existing commitments.

My advice for taking on big adventures is to remember what you've already discovered via smaller adventures: you are capable of more than you think. Be confident enough to pick the right mountain for you, and don't do it to impress anyone, because your best friend did it or because it will be good for your CV. It doesn't have to be productive. Do it because it is the thing you want to do more than anything else in the world. Do it because just thinking about it, just planning it, lights you up, because you are being called to adventure.

Break a big adventure down into manageable steps. As we discovered with Amanda Challans when she used adventure to deal with ME, breaking seemingly impossible tasks into small chunks makes them easier to tackle. Use this technique to plan and prepare for a huge challenge as well as during the journey. When I decided to lead the first women to row around Britain, having very little experience at sea and having only rowed at university on flatwater rivers and canals, I broke the task into components. I didn't think, I've got to prepare everything for a record-breaking mission in an environment I have little experience of. Instead, I figured out I needed a boat, a crew and a mentor. I focused on these three main aspects, knowing that all the other details would shake down from them.

Another important step on the path to planning a big adventure is to be mindful of costs. The single biggest reason expeditions fail is money. Every year, I see so many people fail to start their big adventures because they can't raise the money or lose momentum while trying. I don't want to limit your dreams, but you do have to be realistic about what you'll need to do to get to the starting line. In some ways, getting there will be your biggest challenge.

And, finally, like almost every aspect of life, the most challenging as well as the best part of adventuring is the people. The outcome of your adventure will depend heavily on whether you find the right team and share the same goals. Some adventures are impossible without the expert skills others can bring, like Alan Creedon's crossing of the Irish Sea. You are welcome to use the Explorers Connect 'Join A Team' networking service that links up would-be adventurers, support teams and mentors. In my experience, finding the right team can be the critical step after which big adventures start to really take shape; finding those like-minded teammates or supporters can be the difference between making the adventure a reality or not.

We've seen throughout these pages that adventure is accessible and important for everyone. There is a place for both small everyday adventure as well as epic once-in-a-lifetime challenges. There's also a place for it no matter our age. The first year of setting up Explorers Connect was the same year a sixteen-year-old schoolgirl was attempting to become the youngest to walk to the South Pole (she made it the following year in 2011). It was also then that an eighty-five-year-old grandfather put together a team to raft across the Atlantic (they also arrived the following year after sixty-six days at sea and 2,800 miles on a raft made of pipes).

Although adventure doesn't have to be this big or record-breaking, these feats made me realise I had no intention of hanging up my hiking boots anytime soon, if ever. Adventure is intrinsic; it's too fundamental to who we are as humans to 'grow out of it'. I never want to grow out of adventure; for me, rather than growing old gracefully or disgracefully, I'd rather grow old adventurously. And some exploratory research supports the value of adventure for elderly adults in terms of boosting wellbeing. A 2012 New Zealand study found outdoor adventures that included challenging physical activity, social engagement and the natural environment gave pensioners a boost in physical and mental wellbeing. The study stated that 'the research supports adventure participation as a successful ageing strategy that is relatively low cost, community based, has many preventative health benefits, builds communities and embraces the environment.'

Getting older can also act as a catalyst for achieving adventurous goals. Let me demonstrate this with one final story of adventure, about Paddy, who made a bucket list that included 'sleeping under the stars' shortly before her eighty-eighth birthday. Her friend Astrid Shepherd is a regular at Explorers Connect gatherings, and she told me how she helped Paddy achieve her adventurous dream in 2016. On the night of Paddy's birthday, Astrid and the staff and residents of the care home where Paddy lived sat around a fire drinking hot chocolate, singing campfire songs, listening to poems and toasting marshmallows. When the non-campers went back inside, Astrid, Paddy and Astrid's mum (who'd been Paddy's friend for forty years) settled down outside for the night. Astrid is an experienced camper and had brought all the right kit and expertise to make sure the trio were confident and warm for the night ahead. 'I'm not sure Paddy slept a wink,' said Astrid. 'She clung onto my hand most of the night with excitement, looking up at the stars in wonder, and slept the whole of the following morning to make up for her sleepless excitement.' The way Astrid had given Paddy such an unforgettable gift still fills me with admiration.

Astrid had arranged the campout to coincide with Paddy's birthday but also Wild Night Out, an annual night of adventure where you push yourself to do something adventurous and importantly bring someone else along with you, giving those who might not normally take the plunge a chance to spend more time adventuring. It could be a late-night feast on a hilltop with head torches, a night cycle or camping in your garden or in the wilds – whatever fits you; there are no rules. What's important is that we make time for adventure. It is easy to make bucket lists, but busy lives get in the way of achieving them. Committing to a night of adventure, a date in the diary, gives you a focus. And once you've started, once you've reminded yourself of how fun and rewarding adventure is, I'm hoping you won't stop.

Astrid had been inspired by adventure and was passing the contagion on. She joined Explorers Connect following a break-up and redundancy, and since then she has embarked on snowboarding, scuba diving, climbing, abseiling, high-rope walking, foraging, learning navigation skills, hill walking, scrambling and camping (with and without a tent), and she has cooked many a meal over open fires as part of the community. She also volunteers with other members of Explorers Connect to help disadvantaged kids get out on adventures too.

For Astrid, like so many of the adventurers featured in this book, both those who've embarked on bold expeditions and those who've discovered the benefits of adventure from small and frequent outings, there has been much joy and meaning discovered as a result of living a more adventurous life. And that's important to remember: adventures, although rejuvenating, exciting and enjoyable, are more than your average holiday; they're purposeful, challenging and rewarding. Crucially, there tends to be a 'why' behind them. In that sense, adventure is the difference between trying an hour of stand-up paddleboarding one afternoon during a beach holiday and committing to a stand-up-paddleboarding journey along the coast to a predetermined location. The sense of purpose gives structure, the grit in the oyster, meaning you'll keep going rather than stop as soon as it's a little uncomfortable. And it'll give you so much more than wonder, joy and meaning (although those things are greatly beneficial in themselves) – it'll give you a different perspective on life, more empathy in relationships, more self-belief in your capabilities, and the chance to become your best self and live your dreams. Only by finding the limits of what is possible and stretching ourselves can we become the best we can be. It is the only way to achieve our full potential – by challenging our boundaries, risking defeat and going on anyway.

Epilogue

Adventure Revolution

'Because in the end, you won't remember the time you spent working in the office and mowing the lawn. Climb that goddamn mountain!'

Jack Kerouac

I want to spark a revolution that encourages us all to make more time for adventure in our daily lives, to prioritise adventure more. I believe an Adventure Revolution will make society happier and healthier. And to do that I need your help.

My one hope is that once you've finished reading this book, you will put it down and go on an adventure – no matter how big or small – something you otherwise might not have done. Then, if you find that adventure has helped you in some way, whether it's simply to hit the refresh button or perhaps in a more life-changing way, I'd really love for you to take one other person out on adventure. In doing so, we can start an inspiration contagion – an Adventure Revolution.

Having read this book, you will hopefully, like me, agree that we could all benefit from experiencing more adventure, whether it be going on huge overseas expeditions or doing more exploration in the evenings and weekends close to home. Because only by trying new experiences, by leaving our comfort zone and embracing uncertainty, can we truly find out what we're capable of and become the best versions of ourselves.

Certainly, adventure has changed my life for the better, and I've seen it do the same for countless others too. Before adventure, I was fearful, anxious and lacking in confidence. But adventure gave me the inner strength to stretch beyond what I knew. And once you've stood on top of a mountain, you realise what you are capable of; you see yourself and the world differently – there's no going back, just like Kerouac knew. My couple of decades of adventuring has shown me that it's what we bring back from adventure that matters as much as the in-the-moment experience itself. Adventure has benefits that last long beyond the moment, because we return with so much treasure and so many lessons that we can apply as we continue on our life journeys.

Now, whenever I am about to turn away from a challenge, I ask myself, What's the worst that can happen? And I remember that the worst is usually something I can withstand, and the reward is worth the risk.

I've learnt to let go of the stifling and life-limiting fear of failure and acknowledge that I can do much more than I thought I could. I want that for my child. And I want that for you too. To return from an adventure and think, If I can do this, then what else am I capable of? This is why adventure is so often a watershed moment for us all. What if I fail? transforms into, What if I succeed?

The new and improved you is a gift to the world. I've seen adventure nourish people into becoming more outward-looking, adaptable, compassionate, motivated, brave and resilient. And, let's face it, right now we need more people with these kinds of qualities in the world. We are living in a time when we are experiencing monumental environmental, economic and social change at great speed, and with that comes great challenge. We need adventurous people to confront uncomfortable questions, face uncertainty and be willing to put up with the tough stages in between transition.

From bringing our own personal gifts back to the world, having grown from adventure, we can make a difference to our lives and our worlds. A wonderful side effect of going on adventures is that it fosters a respect and care for the natural environment. You learn to appreciate it in all its wildness. I've rarely met an adventurer who is not passionate about protecting the wilderness that we have left. At the end of 2020, scientists from the Weizmann Institute of Science in Israel announced that the weight of human-made objects (all the plastic, bricks, concrete, etc.) had exceeded that of living things (all the animals, microbes and plants) on the planet for the first time. The significance was symbolic of the way we've transformed our environment; we have reached a point at which it is time for us to assess the balance between the living world and modern humanity, our past and our potential future.

Looking back at our evolutionary history, the speed at which the hunter-gatherer world became the agricultural, then industrial, then the information age has brought us to a place of exponential change. And the accompanying decline in our mental health demonstrates the need to find an achievable antidote. The nature effect is part of the equation, but I believe it's the Adventure Effect that is needed to really push us over the finishing line and embrace the future – to not just cope better but to flourish.

I hope this book has shown you how adventure can help us and how adventure can make us feel better, think better and do better. Whether in small, regular doses or big, challenging steps, adventure is what this world needs. One bold step at a time.

Where do we go from here?

There are promising signs that an Adventure Revolution is already beginning. For example, a report published in 2013 by George Washington University and the Adventure Travel Trade Association stated that growth in adventure tourism had accelerated at 65 per cent annually since 2009.

Educational and therapeutic organisations are also offering more adventure alternatives. In 2001, researcher Aram Attarian confirmed that overall participation in outdoor adventure-education programmes had increased in the fifteen years previous. Participation in organised adventure programmes designed to improve wellbeing is increasing too, especially for women and older adults. Researchers in 1998 found that up to 70,000 people participate in the more than 700 wilderness-experience programmes in the United States each year. These initiatives were classified as 'wilderness experiences', but a closer look shows that the majority of them included expedition-style journeys or challenges – in other words, adventures. We don't have the data to put an exact figure on the number of people participating in adventure programmes today, but it's fair to say it seems to be on the increase, at least in the USA.

In the UK, there's still a long way to go, but the recent growth of social prescribing within the NHS means that more people are being prescribed adventure as physical and mental therapy, like Sam who joined The Wave Project in Cornwall in chapter two. As we've learnt, going on adventures can be the best and most natural medicine there is. What's more, adventure is easier to prescribe than duty-bound healthy living; after all, we've been trying that for years. The benefits of healthy living – sufficient exercise, eating a nutritious and balanced diet, and getting plenty of sleep – are well documented. We don't lack the understanding or awareness to follow these simple rules for a healthier, longer, happier life. Yet, we often don't stick to these rules for healthy living because they don't feel especially enjoyable or exciting, unlike adventure, which does. Adventure can be playful, varied and purposeful, so we are more likely to want to weave it into our lifestyle as a result.

Now, as well as getting out there and living more adventurously, to spark a true Adventure Revolution, we need to spread the word. We need to take friends and family members with us. But we also need to encourage and enable our policy-makers and institutions to include adventure in their planning too. This should include more interventions like those seen in social prescribing and adventure therapy to deal with the physical- and mental-wellbeing problems our societies face. But more than that, we need to look at prevention and building for the future rather than treating the symptoms. For true revolution, systemic change is needed throughout our communities.

Adventure education has been decimated in the UK over the last forty years. For example, research in 2018 by the University of Stirling found there were 123 residential outdoor adventure centres in Scotland in 1982, more than seventy of them run by local authorities. By 2018, that had fallen to sixty-four centres, with less than a dozen owned by councils. And by 2020 there were just seven council centres. These centres offer children a unique opportunity to immerse themselves in adventure in wild locations that cannot be achieved in city parks or day trips. Such centres were routinely run and subsidised in the 1970s by local government so that all children could attend. Over the years, funding has been cut to the point that most of those remaining are expected to be profit-making in order to survive. This fundamental shift in values, from funding outdoor adventure for children to councils using these centres to produce profit, is a reflection of wider educational shifts. I think we should be reallocating resources away from ever-increasing testing and supervision to giving children more freedom to grow and experience adventure, including at residential centres. If we banned homework for primary kids and gave them local adventure missions instead, we would surely end up with more engaged, resilient and uniquely talented children in the future. We would even achieve better academic results, as found in the research in chapter two by the Education Endowment Foundation. Each time we add an extra hour to a child's school day or homework or coerce them into another adult-directed extracurricular activity, we deprive them of opportunities to play, explore, reflect and experience on their own terms. The evidence is clear: we just need to tip the balance into active reform. The good news is that this tide is starting to turn too; in 2014, the British government made it mandatory to include 'outdoor adventurous activities' in primary education.

Similarly, the allocation of funding for traditional team sports should be re-examined. Sport is an important part of any community, but it does not reach everyone. Hard-to-reach groups of children and adults are more likely to engage in the less-competitive, less-rule-bound adventure alternatives that offer managed risk-taking and result in better behaviour and sense of community.

As much as we'd love every child and adult to have regular access to wild natural spaces, when this is not possible the alternative is to rethink how we design our urban environments. If we consider adventurous physical activity a mainstream intervention for positive mental health, we should design our everyday environments to provide opportunities for adventure. This could include design that promotes play close to home by closing more residential roads to traffic. It could include putting up climbing walls at public buildings and encouraging parkour in all spaces. We need to provide and create more playful cities for both children and adults, spaces that encourage physical activity, variety and challenge. Exercise scientists, health professionals, planners, engineers and psychologists should collaborate in co-designing environments and playscapes that facilitate adventure.

Increasingly, our societies need to assign monetary values to every aspect of our lives in order for us to appreciate them. As much as I instinctively dislike this, sometimes it is a case of 'if you can't beat 'em, join 'em'. It is the job of researchers to communicate the value of adventure to our society. For example, if we are able to quantify the economic impact of lost workdays due to stress, and how this can be alleviated through resources spent on adventure provision, we can prove it is not just morally the right answer but economically sensible. I used to argue that much of the value of living adventurously is not measurable, but my research across multiple disciplines shows that this is no longer good enough. We need to fund further research and focus on the priorities that are identified. We need to give policy-makers facts to work with. We also need more research into how we design adventure to make it as cost-effective for wellbeing as possible, to recognise adventure not just as a therapy but as a necessity for all and produce methodologies in how to use adventure to reach our potential.

We need to rebrand adventure and its essential place in twenty-first-century living – to understand that adventure builds a love of life and a deep appreciation for the world and others. Adventure is not a frivolous escape but an essential experience from which we learn how to participate in society, to find out what we have to give. Adventure can build a better us and a better world.

We are now at a tipping point. We have the evidence: both of the harm done by this current state of affairs and of the many benefits of living adventurously. And we have the opportunity, not least because adventure can be provided at a low cost, an important factor at this time of economic stress. We have the means, motive and opportunity. Now we need the will. Things can't be changed overnight, but we must start somewhere. This book is a first step, providing clues to how and why we should rewild our lives, and an attempt to raise the level of the debate. The goal is nothing less than to kick-start the creation of a new way of life for ourselves and our children.

One final piece of advice: don't burn yourselves out. Be a part-time revolutionary. Spread the word, consider what's at stake, take action where you can, but save the other half of yourself for adventuring. It's not enough to rally for change; we must also enjoy what we have while we can. Get out to hike, bike, swim, climb, explore. Follow your own rules while respecting those around you and the environment. Leave your comfort zone, discover what you're capable of, be in awe of your achievements and your teammates, find your meaning in life. The world needs people who are fully engaged and truly alive to make a difference among their friends, families and communities.

People often ask me which expedition was my favourite or 'the best', and it will always be that first one, because no adventure since has had such a mind-altering effect. My very first big adventure – my trip to Africa – truly changed my life. Had I remained compliant and not stepped outside of my comfort zone, I would probably have ended up with a sensible but unfulfilling and inauthentic career. That first adventure shifted my view of the world and my place in it. So, as much as the adventures since then have enabled me to grow, that was the most transformational adventure for me. The question is, which adventure will be the one that changes your life?

Acknowledgements

Thank you to my editor Holly Harley for helping me make the book the best it can be and to my agent Cathryn Summerhayes for sharing my passion and championing the cause. Dr Alan Ewert and Dr Tom Kemp, I'm hugely grateful for your excellent notes and wisdom. (And thanks to Tom for breaking the rules all those years ago.) To Kate Davies, Libi Bowles, Nic Albert and Martin Toseland, thank you for your feedback on my draft manuscripts and for the brutal honesty when it was necessary.

Special gratitude is owed to those who shared their journeys with me: Ade Adepitan, Kelvyn James, Joe Taylor, Jen, Phil Coates, Danny, Beth Thomas, Amanda Challans, Penny Challans, Benedict Allen, Andy Kirkpatrick, Richie Bates, Paula McGuire, Freyja, Amina Smith-Gul, Stu Skinner, Alex Staniforth, Alan Creedon and Alice and her mum.

Important contributions were also made by Eric Brymer, Emma Barrett, Anita Kerwin-Nye, Chris Loynes, John Allan,

Simon Beames, Chris Kay, Gill Pomfret, Paula Reid, Jenny Edwards, Honor Wilson-Fletcher and Andy Barnett.

My darling Jackson, thank you for letting mummy write this book, even on sunny days when we both wanted to go outside and have adventures together instead. And Jim, thank you for your support and advice, without which I would never have finished this book, and, in general, for continuing to put up with me. Finally, I'm so grateful to everyone I've been on an adventure with – let's start planning some more.

References

Chapter One

The Hero with a Thousand Faces, Joseph Campbell, Pantheon Books, 1949

Chapter Two

Last Child in the Woods: Saving Our Children from Nature-deficit Disorder, Richard Louv, Atlantic Books, 2010

'The health benefits of the great outdoors: a systematic review and meta-analysis of greenspace exposure and health outcomes', Caoimhe Twohig-Bennett and Andy Jones, *Environmental Research Journal*, 2018, 166:628-637

'Effect of forest bathing trips on human immune function', Qing Li, *Environmental Health and Preventive Medicine Journal*, 2010, 15(1):9-17

'Effect of phytoncide from trees on human natural killer cell function', Qing Li, et al., *International Journal of Immunopathology and Pharmacology*, 2009, 22(4):951-959

'Identification and characterization of a novel anti-inflammatory lipid isolated from Mycobacterium vaccae, a soil-derived bacterium with immunoregulatory and stress resilience properties', David Smith, et al., *Psychopharmacology*, 2019, 236(5):1653–1670

'Mind-wandering and alterations to default mode network connectivity when listening to naturalistic versus artificial sounds', Cassandra D. Gould van Praag, et al., *Scientific Reports*, 2017, 7:45273

'Can nature make us more caring? Effects of immersion in nature on intrinsic aspirations and generosity', Netta Weinstein, et al., *Personality and Social Psychology Bulletin*, 2009, 35(10):1315 –1329

Biophilia, Edward Wilson, Harvard University Press, 1984

'Adventurous Physical Activity Environments: A Mainstream Intervention for Mental Health', Peter Clough, et al., *Sports Medicine*, 2016, 46(7):963–968

Women in Adventure: Mental Wellbeing Survey Report, Hetty Key, 2019

'Mental health benefits of outdoor adventures: Results from two pilot studies', Michael Mutz and Johannes Müller, *Journal of Adolescence*, 2016, 49:105–14

'Adventure Education and Outward Bound: out-of-class experiences that make a lasting difference', John Hattie, et al., *Review of Educational Research*, 1997, 67(1):43–87

Outdoor adventure pursuits: foundations, models and theories, Alan Ewert, Gorsuch Scarisbrick Pub, 1989

'Testing the Adventure Model: Empirical Support for a Model of Risk Recreation Participation', Alan Ewert and Steve Hollenhorst, *Journal of Leisure Research*, 1989, 21(2):124–139

'Health and Wellbeing in an Outdoor and Adventure Sports Context', John Allan, et al., *Sports*, 2020, 8(4): 50

'Whatever Does Not Kill Us: Cumulative Lifetime Adversity, Vulnerability, and Resilience', Mark Seery, et al., *Journal of Personality and Social Psychology*, 2010, 99(6):1025–41

Outward Bound Social Impact Report, 2017

Surf therapy: the long-term impact. An independent longitudinal evaluation of the impact of The Wave Project on vulnerable young people 2013–2017, Hannah Devine-Wright and Cath Godfrey, 2018

'An outcome evaluation of the implementation of the Outward Bound Singapore five-day "intercept" program', Rebecca Ang, *Journal of Adolescence*, 2014, 37(6):771-8

'Residential wilderness programs: the role of social support in influencing self-evaluations of male adolescents', Emily Cook, *Adolescence*, 2008, 43(172):751-74.

Education Endowment Foundation's Teaching and Learning Toolkit, 2018

World Happiness Report, John Helliwell, Richard Layard and Jeffrey Sachs, 2015. New York: Sustainable Development Solutions Network.

Flourish: A Visionary New Understanding of Happiness and Well-being, Martin Seligman, Nicholas Brealey Publishing, 2011

'The broaden-and-build theory of positive emotions', Barbara L. Fredrickson, *Philosophical Transactions of the Royal Society London*, 2004, *359*(1449):1367–1378

'Exploring the psychology of extended-period expeditionary adventurers: going knowingly into the unknown', Paula Reid and Hanna Kampman, *Psychology of Sport & Exercise*, 2020, 46:101608

'Leading a meaningful life at older ages and its relationship with social engagement, prosperity, health, biology, and time use', Andrew Steptoe and Daisy Fancourt, *Proceedings of the National Academy of Sciences*, 2019, 116(4):201814723

'Purpose, Mood, and Pleasure in Predicting Satisfaction Judgments', Ed Diener, et al., *Social Indicators Research*, 2012, 105: 333–341

Chapter Three

The Hunter-Gatherer Way: Putting Back the Apple, Ffyona Campbell, 2012

'In Britain's Playgrounds, "Bringing in Risk" to Build Resilience', Ellen Barry, *New York Times*, March 2018

A survey by Keele University researcher Sarah Thomson reported by BBC Education, http://news.bbc.co.uk/1/hi/

education/1060708.stm, December 2000 (accessed 3 January 2021)

'Mont Blanc: French mayor to fine badly prepared climbers', *The Local*, https://www.thelocal.fr/20170817/mont-blanc-french-mayor-to-fine-ill-prepared-climbers, 17 August 2017 (accessed 3 January 2021)

Feral: Rewilding the Land, Sea and Human Life, George Monbiot, Penguin, 2014

'National Human Activity Pattern Survey: A Resource for Assessing Exposure to Environmental Pollutants', Neil Edward Klepeis, et al., *Journal of Exposure Analysis and Environmental Epidemiology*, 2001, 11(3):231-52

United Nations News, quoting the 2007 Revision of World Urbanization Prospects https://news.un.org/en/story/2008/02/250402-half-global-population-will-live-cities-end-year-predicts-un (accessed 3 January 2021)

'Paleolithic nutrition revisited: a twelve-year retrospective on its nature and implications', S.B. Eaton, et al, *European Journal of Clinical Nutrition*, 1997, 51(4):207-16

'Cardiovascular Disease Resulting from a Diet and Lifestyle at Odds With Our Paleolithic Genome: How to Become a 21st-Century Hunter-Gatherer', James O'Keefe Jr and Loren Cordain, *Mayo Clinic Proceedings*, 2004, 79(1):101-8

https://www.cdc.gov/heartdisease/facts.htm (accessed 3 January 2021)

https://news.sky.com/story/seven-charts-on-the-uks-obesity-problem-11583981 (accessed 3 January 2021)

https://www.diabetesaustralia.com.au/about-diabetes/diabetes-in-australia/ (accessed 3 January 2021)

'The western diet and lifestyle and diseases of civilization', Pedro Carrera-Bastos, et al., *Research Reports in Clinical Cardiology*, 2011, 2(2):2-15

The Story of the Human Body: Evolution, Health and Disease, Daniel Lieberman, Penguin, 2014

https://www.bbc.com/news/health-54531075 (accessed 3 January 2021)

'Acute effects of sauna bathing on cardiovascular function', Tanjanlina Laukkanen, et al., *Journal of Human Hypertension*, 2018, 32(2):129-138

'Sauna Bathing and Incident Hypertension: A Prospective Cohort Study', Francesco Zaccardi, et al., *American Journal of Hypertension*, 2017, 30(11):1120-1125

'Association Between Sauna Bathing and Fatal Cardiovascular and All-Cause Mortality Events', Tanjanlina Laukkanen, et al., *Cardiology*, 2015, 175(4):542-8

'Fasting: Molecular Mechanisms and Clinical Applications', Valter D. Longo and Mark P. Mattson, *Cell Metabolism*, 2014, 19(2):181-192

Way of the Iceman: How the Wim Hof Method Creates Radiant, Longterm Health, Wim Hof, Dragon Door Publications, 2017

Sapiens: A Brief History of Humankind, Yuval Noah Harari, Vintage, 2015

The State of Mental Health in America, https://www.mhanational.org/issues/state-mental-health-america (accessed 3 January 2021)

'Stressed nation: 74% of UK "overwhelmed or unable to cope" at some point in the past year', Mental Health Foundation, YouGov, 2018, https://www.mentalhealth.org.uk/news/stressed-nation-74-uk-overwhelmed-or-unable-cope-some-point-past-year (accessed 3 January 2021)

Adult Psychiatric Morbidity Survey: Survey of Mental Health and Wellbeing, England, 2014, https://webarchive.nationalarchives.gov.uk/20180328140249/http://digital.nhs.uk/catalogue/PUB21748

'Evolutionary well-being: the Paleolithic model', Francis Heylighen, *Evolution, Cognition and Complexity*, 2010, https://slidetodoc.com/evolutionary-wellbeing-the-paleolithic-model-francis-heylighen-evolution/ (accessed 3 January 2021)

Brain Rules, Updated and Expanded: 12 Principles for Surviving and Thriving at Work, Home, and School, John Medina, Pear Press, 2014

Wild Harvest, Hope Bourne, Exmoor Books, 2001

'Lifestyle and nutritional imbalances associated with Western diseases: causes and consequences of chronic systemic low-grade inflammation in an evolutionary context', Begoña Ruiz -Núñez, et al., *Journal of Nutritional Biochemistry*, 2013, 24(7):1183-201

Chapter Four

'Adventure education and resilience: the double-edged sword', James Neil and Katica Dias, *Journal of Adventure Education and Outdoor Learning*, 2001, 1(2):35-42

From Surviving to Thriving: Trajectories of Resilience in University Inductees following Outdoor Adventure (OA) Residential Programmes, John Allan and Jim McKenna, 2020

'Outdoor Adventure Builds Resilient Learners for Higher Education: A Quantitative Analysis of the Active Components of Positive Change', John Allan and Jim McKenna, *Sports (Basel)*, 2019, 7(5): 122

'Scouts and Guides at lower risk of mental illness later in life – study', *Guardian*, 2016, https://www.theguardian.com/ society/2016/nov/10/scouts-and-guides-at-lower-risk-of -mental-illness-in-later-life-study (accessed 3 January 2021)

Mental Health and Resilience Report, Outward Bound, 2019, https: //www.outwardbound.org.uk/assets/pdf/uploads/Trust%20 general/Young-Peoples-Mental-Health-and-Resilience-Report.pdf (accessed 3 January 2021)

The Role of Residential Rehab in an Integrated Treatment System, National Treatment Agency for Substance Misuse, 2012, https: //webarchive.nationalarchives.gov.uk/20170807160631/http: //www.nta.nhs.uk/uploads/roleofresi-rehab.pdf (accessed 3 January 2021)

'Adventure Therapy Treatment for Young Adult Males Struggling with Addictions', Keith Russell, et al., *Journal of Health Service Psychology*, 2020, 46:13-20

'Wilderness family therapy: an innovative treatment approach for problem youth', Scott Bandoroff and David Scherer, *Journal of Child and Family Studies*, 1994, 3(2):175-191 'Adventure therapy for child, adolescent, and young adult cancer patients: a systematic review', Ying Tung Chan, et al., *Supportive Care in Cancer*, 2020, 29(1):35-48

'Disability, inclusive adventurous training and adapted sport: two soldiers' stories of involvement', David Carless, et al., *Psychology of Sport and Exercise*, 2013, 15(1):124-131

'The promise of river running as a therapeutic medium for veterans coping with post-traumatic stress disorder', Daniel Dustin, et al., *Therapeutic Recreation Journal*, 2011, 45(4):326 -340

'Climbing towards recovery: investigating physically injured combat veterans' psychosocial responses to scaling Mt. Kilimanjaro', Shaunna Burke and Andrea Utley, *Disability and Rehabilitation*, 2012, 35(9):732-9

Wilderness Therapy for Women: The Power of Adventure, Ellen Cole, et al., Harrington Park Press, 1994

'A Meta-Analysis of Adventure Therapy Outcomes and Moderators', Daniel Bowen and James Neill, *The Open Psychology Journal*, 2013, 6(1):28-53

Chapter Five

'Parents investigated for neglect after letting kids walk home alone', Donna St George, *Washington Post*, 2015, https://www.washingtonpost.com/local/education/maryland-couple-want-free-range-kids-but-not-all-do/2015/01/14/d406c0be-9c0f-11e4-bcfb-059ec7a93ddc_story.html (accessed 3 January 2021)

'I let my 9-year-old ride the subway alone. I got labeled the "world's worst mom"', Lenore Skenazy, *Washington Post*, 2015, https://www.washingtonpost.com/posteverything/wp/2015/01/16/i-let-my-9-year-old-ride-the-subway-alone-i-got-labeled-the-worlds-worst-mom/(accessed 3 January 2021)

Childhood and nature: a survey on changing relationships with nature across generations, report commissioned by Natural England and published by England Marketing, 2009, http://publications.naturalengland.org.uk/publication/5853658314964992

'Three-quarters of UK children spend less time outdoors than prison inmates – survey', Damian Carrington, *Guardian*, 2016, https://www.theguardian.com/environment/2016/mar/25/three-quarters-of-uk-children-spend-less-time-outdoors-than-prison-inmates-survey (accessed 3 January 2021)

'Why our children need to get outside and engage with nature', Jon Henley, *Guardian*, 2010, https://www.theguardian.com/lifeandstyle/2010/aug/16/childre-nature-outside-play-health (accessed 3 January 2021)

Play England (2008), quoted in the *Guardian*, www.guardian.co.uk/education/2008/aug/03/schools.children (accessed 3 January 2021)

'Urban Children's Access to Their Neighbourhood: Changes Over Three Generations', Sanford Gaster, *Environment and Behaviour*, 1991, quoted by Richard Louv, p. 123 of *Last Child in the Woods*, 2005

One False Move: A Study of Children's Independent Mobility, Mayer Hillman, John Adams and John Whitelegg, London: Policy Studies Institute, 1990

Natural Childhood, Stephen Moss, National Trust, https://nt.global.ssl.fastly.net/documents/read-our-natural-childhood-report.pdf (accessed 3 January 2021)

'Does Being Bored Make Us More Creative?', Sandi Mann and Rebekah Cadman, *Creativity Research Journal*, 2014, 26(2):165–173

'Approaching Novel Thoughts: Understanding Why Elation and Boredom Promote Associative Thought More than Distress and Relaxation', Karen Gasper and Brianna Middlewood, *Journal of Experimental Social Psychology*, 2014, 52:50–57

Public Space and the Culture of Childhood, Gill Valentine, Routledge, 2004

Play, a report by the All-Party Parliamentary Group for a Fit and Healthy Childhood, Helen Clark, et al., 2015

Not a Risk Averse Society, Rob Wheway, 2008

Council for Learning Outside the Classroom, https://www. lotc.org.uk/why/risk-challenge-and-adventure/ (accessed 3 January 2021)

'Declining Student Resilience: A Serious Problem for Colleges', Peter Gray, https://www.psychologytoday.com/gb/blog/ freedom-learn/201509/declining-student-resilience-serious-problem-colleges (accessed 3 January 2021)

'Helicopter Parenting, Self-Control, and School Burnout among Emerging Adults', Hayley Love, et al., *Journal of Child and Family Studies*, 2019, 29:327-337

'No fear: growing up in a risk averse society', Tim Gill, Calouste Gulbenkian Foundation, 2007

'Jumping off and being careful: children's strategies of risk management in everyday life', Pia Christensen and Miguel Mikkelsen, *Sociology of Health & Illness*, 2008, 30(1):112 -30

'Making Playgrounds a Little More Dangerous', Richard Schiffman, *New York Times*, 2019, https://www.nytimes.com/ 2019/05/10/well/family/adventure-playgrounds-junk-play-grounds.html (accessed 3 April 2021)

'What Is the Relationship between Risky Outdoor Play and Health in Children? A Systematic Review', Mariana Brussoni, et al., *International Journal of Environmental Research and Public Health*, 2015, 12(6):6423-6454

'Change of School Playground Environment on Bullying: A Randomized Controlled Trial', Victoria Farmer, et al., *Pediatrics*, 2017, 139(5):3072

'Risk taking and novelty seeking in adolescence: introduction to part I', Ann E. Kelley, Terri Schochet, Charles F. Landry, *Annals of the New York Academy of Sciences*, 2004, 1021:27-32

'Age of onset of mental disorders: a review of recent literature', Ronald Kessler, et al., *Current Opinion in Psychiatry*, 2007, 20(4):359-364

'Risky Play' and 'Lessons' blogs by Andy Kirkpatrick, https://www.andy-kirkpatrick.com/blog/view/risky_play and https://www.andy-kirkpatrick.com/blog/view/lessons (accessed 3 January 2021)

Chapter Six

River grades as explained by British Canoeing https://www.britishcanoeing.org.uk/uploads/documents/British-Canoeing-Environmental-Definitions-Deployment-Guidance-for-Instructors-Coaches-Leaders-Apr18-v1-1.pdf (accessed 3 January 2021)

Extreme Fear: The Science of Your Mind in Danger, Jeff Wise, St. Martin's Press, 2011

'Extreme sports are good for your health: a phenomenological understanding of fear and anxiety in extreme sport', Eric Brymer and Robert Schweitzer, *Journal of Health Psychology*, 2012, 18(4):477-487

'Extreme dude! A phenomenological perspective on the extreme sport experience', Eric Brymer, *University of Wollongong Theses Collection*, 2005

Extreme: Why Some People Thrive at the Limits, Emma Barrett and Paul Martin, OUP Oxford, 2014

Paula McGuire presentation for TEDx Glasgow in 2015, www.youtube.com/watch?v=W7kZWmw3JxY (accessed 3 January 2021)

Chapter Seven

Quicksilver: Adventure Games, Initiative Problems, Trust Activities and a Guide to Effective Leadership, Karl Rohnke and Steve Butler, Kendall Hunt Publishing Company, 1995

'The relation of strength of stimulus to rapidity of habit-formation', Robert Yerkes and John Dodson, *Journal of Comparative Neurology and Psychology*, 1908, 18(5):459-482

Mindset: Changing the Way You Think to Fulfil Your Potential, Carol Dweck, Robinson, updated 2017

Chapter Eight

'Social Relationships and Health: A Flashpoint for Health Policy', Debra Umberson and Jennifer Karas Montez, *Journal of Health and Social Behaviour*, 2010, 51(Suppl):54-66

The Harvard Study of Adult Development, ongoing study at https://www.adultdevelopmentstudy.org/ (accessed 3 January 2021)

'Families at leisure outdoors: well-being through adventure', Gill Pomfret and Peter Varley, *Leisure Studies*, 2019, 38(4):494-508

'How many hours does it take to make a friend?', Jeffrey Hall, *Journal of Social and Personal Relationships*, 2018, 36(4):1278 -1296

'Pain As Social Glue: Shared Pain Increases Cooperation', Brock Bastian, Jolanda Jetten and Laura J. Ferris, *Psychological Science*, 2014, 25(11):2079-2085

'The Social Dimension of Stress Reactivity: Acute Stress Increases Prosocial Behavior in Humans', Bernadette von Dawans, et al., *Psychological Science*, 2012, 23(6):651-60

'Effects of Acute Stress on Social Behavior in Women', Bernadette von Dawans, et al., Psychoneuroendocrinology, 2018, 99:137 -144

Daring Greatly: How the Courage to Be Vulnerable Transforms the Way We Live, Love, Parent, and Lead, Brené Brown, Penguin Random House USA, 2015

Chapter Nine

'Why the Hadza are Still Hunter-Gatherers', Frank Marlowe, in *Ethnicity, Hunter-Gatherers, and the 'Other': Association or Assimilation in Africa*, Smithsonian Institution Scholarly Press, 2002

'Notes on Hadza cosmology: epeme, objects and rituals', Thea Skaanes, *Hunter Gatherer Research*, 2015, 1(2):247-267

'The Giving Environment: Another Perspective on the Economic System of Gatherer-Hunters', Nurit Bird-David, *Current Anthropology*, 1990, 31(2):189-196

Bushmen: Kalahari Hunter-Gatherers and Their Descendants, Alan Barnard, Cambridge University Press, 2019

The Bushmen, Alf Wannenburgh, Chartwell Books Inc, 1989

Free to Learn: Why Unleashing the Instinct to Play Will Make Our Children Happier, More Self-Reliant, and Better Students for Life, Peter Gray, Basic Books, 2013

'The biology of happiness: Chasing pleasure and human destiny', Ladislav Kováč, *Science and Society*, 2012, 13(4):297-302

Flow: The Psychology of Happiness, Mihaly Csikszentmihalyi, Ebury Publishing, 2002

'The search for freedom in extreme sports: a phenomenological exploration, Eric Brymer and Robert D. Schweitzer', *Psychology of Sport and Exercise*, 2013, 14(6):865-873

'Evoking the ineffable: the phenomenology of extreme sports', Eric Brymer and Robert D. Schweitzer, *Psychology of Consciousness: Theory, Research, and Practice*, 2017, 4(1):63-74

'A phenomenological investigation of the experience of taking part in "Extreme Sports"', Carla Willig, *Journal of Health Psychology*, 2008, 13(5):690-702

'The Surprising Science Behind Why Every Cyclist Freaking Loves Getting Air', Gloria Liu, *Bicycling* magazine, 2019, https://www.bicycling.com/skills-tips/a26683483/psychology-of-jumping-on-a-bike/ (accessed 3 January 2021)

Chapter Eleven

www.parkour.uk (accessed 3 January 2021)

'Outdoor adventure and successful ageing', Mike Boyes, *Ageing and Society*, 2012, 33(4):644-665

'Understanding Educational Expeditions', Simon Beames, Sense Publishers, 2009

'Lifestyle sport, public policy and youth engagement: examining the emergence of parkour', Paul Gilchrist and Belinda Wheaton, *International Journal of Sport Policy and Politics*, 2011, 3(1):109-131

Epilogue

'Human-made objects to outweigh living things', Helen Briggs, BBC News, December 2020, https://www.bbc.co.uk/news/science-environment-55239668 (accessed 3 January 2021)

Adventure Tourism Market Study by the George Washington University conducted in partnership with the Adventure Travel Trade Association 2013

'Trends in Outdoor Adventure Education', Aram Attarian, *Journal of Experiential Education*, 2001, 24(3), 141-149

'Adventure Therapy As a Complementary and Alternative Therapy', Denise Mitten, in *Coming of Age: The Evolving Field of Adventure Therapy*, Association for Experiential Education, 2004

'Seeing the wood from the trees: constructionism and constructivism for outdoor and experiential education', Mark F. Leather, *Philosophy of Education Society of Great Britain*, 2012

'The Wilderness Experience Program Industry in the United States: Characteristics and Dynamics', Greg Friese, John C. Hendee and Mike Kinziger, *Journal of Experiential Education*, 1998, 21(1):40-45

'Residential Outdoor Education in Scotland: Change Over Time and the Impacts of Socio-economic Deprivation on Access', Rebecca Davies, University of Stirling, 2018

'Why are Scottish councils closing their outdoor centres?', Christopher Sleight, BBC News, 2020, https://www.bbc.co.uk/news/uk-scotland-51627635 (accessed 3 January 2021)

'Outdoor adventure within primary education', Chris Webber, Leeds Beckett University, 2019

'Beyond risk: the importance of adventure in the everyday life of young people', Eric Brymer and Francesco Feletti, *Annals of Leisure Research*, 2019, 23(2):1-18

'Adventurous Physical Activity Environments: A Mainstream Intervention for Mental Health', Peter Clough, et al., *Sports Medicine*, 2016, 46(7):963-8